I0054216

SMALL GROUP

AND TEAM

COMMUNICATION

Tried-and-True Ideas to Improve Team

Communication and Achieving Superior

Performance

EMMA KELLER

Copyright © 2022 EMMA KELLER

All rights reserved. No part of this book may be reproduced or transmitted in any form or by any means, electronic or mechanical, including photocopying, recording, or by any information storage and retrieval system, without permission in writing from the author.

TABLE OF CONTENTS

————— ◆ ◇ ◆ —————

CHAPTER 1: WHAT SMALL GROUPS ARE

———— ◆◇◆ ————

Today when we talk about a group what are we referring to? Various definitions have been proposed. What for some scholars is the simplest and most comprehensive, says that a group is when "two or more individuals, who have a common social identification, are recognized as a group by at least a third party". The interaction within it is of the face-to-face type and the members perceive themselves as participants in a unity that lasts in time and space. Finally, the group members are involved in at least one common goal.

If we carefully examine our society we will realize that it is made up of a whole group and that these groups are functional to its existence. Thanks to the studies conducted by Anzien and Martin we have an initial classification of human groups, divided into a crowd, the gang (and the gang); the primary group or small group, the secondary group, or medium-large group.

The crowd

Crowds can be considered the most basic form of group. It connotes a lack of common characteristics between several individuals, but rather a simple physical closeness that makes it possible to satisfy the wishes of the individual participants. This is the case of bathers on a beach or young people cheering at a concert.

The crowd situation develops a typical psychological state: the passivity of the people gathered towards everything that has nothing but the immediate satisfaction of their individual motivation; absence or low level of social contacts or human relationships; the contagion of emotions and rapt propagation to the whole of an agitation born in one point; stimulation produced by the presence of the other in massive doses: and which can explode in the form of fleeting and paroxysmal collective actions, marked by the marks of violence or enthusiasm or which can instead induce a collective apathy impermeable to almost all interventions.

Crowd phenomena have been separated from mass phenomena. Certainly, the massive presence of other human beings is an essential cause of some of the behaviors seen in the crowd. But it would be desirable to make use of the term crowd for any spontaneous or conventional meeting of a large number of people and to reserve the expression mass for all phenomena of collective psychology concerning an even greater number of people, who are neither physically united nor reunited: fashion, public opinion, currents of thought... etc.

The band

Crowds are defined by the psychology of simultaneity. A crowd has loneliness in common. The band, on the other hand, has a similarity in common.

The band is very different from the crowd, for the limited number of its members (some units or a few tens), for its longer duration. It is created when a series of individuals, usually adolescents, meet to be together as "we recognize each other as similar". Members tend to harmonize with each other, and all of this gives a sense of security and emotional support.

Life in the gang is short as the psychological growth of individuals undermines the roots of primary function. If, on the other hand, the gang persists, it transforms into a gang and consequently also changes its internal structure, it begins to function as a primary group.

Grouping

When people gather, whether they are small, medium, or large, with a greater or lesser frequency of meetings, with a relative permanence of objectives in the intervals of the meetings, they constitute a grouping.

The objectives of the grouping respond to a common interest of all members. These are partially aware of it, but most of them do not actively take charge of this interest, the members are devoid of ties and contacts. It could be said that their goal is common but that, individually, they have nothing in common; they have not appropriated it. Most associations are of this type.

Other examples can be enumerated in a non-limiting manner: assembly, coalition, collectivity, dormitories, colonies, companies, brotherhoods, fractions, harems, legions, troops, units.

The primary group

This is characterized by the intimate face-to-face association and cooperation that allows the individual to express himself in a personal way and to consider the group as a positive container of his internal world. Its internal structure is divided by roles or at least by a "game of parts" and by the attribution of tasks. The primary group turns out less to norms regulation.

It is rather articulated on unwritten ethics based on norms of behavior relating to normal social coexistence, more specifically concerning the way of relating with the other. However, the unwritten rules are no less binding than the legitimate ones.

The individual spontaneously becomes part of a primary group which for him becomes the group he belongs to in the light of which he must frame his behavior. When the individual no longer feels the rules of the group he belongs to, he no longer adapts his behavior to them; he, therefore, becomes unconventional concerning the group to which he belongs and conformist with respect to any other group whose purposes become a priority for him over the previous ones. This is why the group in which the individual now turns his or her interest is called the reference group.

The Secondary Group

It is characterized by poor personal contact between its members (neutral relationships), the interaction between which is related to the achievement of a specific goal.

Unlike the primary group, in the secondary group, the norms are almost always fixed by a broader and more formal system of relationships, and the interaction between the members in most cases is short-lived and with little personal implication. Among the structural aspects of the group, that of "role" and that of "status" occupy a central position. The role is the behavior that the individual must assume in society.

Having a role leads us to behave in certain ways, and, in the people around us, it evokes certain expectations that are consistent with the position we occupy. The role is formally established, allowing the division of labor between members of the group. This generally facilitates the achievement of the group's purpose and is, therefore, an important motivating factor. Roles help bring order to the existence of the group; in fact, everyone knows what to do and what the tasks of the other members are. Finally, the roles have the function of defining the identity of each member. Having a role undoubtedly contributes to forming one's identity, one's self.

Otherwise, status represents the position that an individual occupies in society. The existence of status differences within a group is due to social confrontation. This consists of a self-evaluation by which individuals compare their abilities with those of others.

The entry of an individual into a group generates the development of a series of processes such as the modification of the concept of self and the mutual interdependence between the members of the group.

Self-concept

When one becomes a member of a group, there are noticeable changes in self-concept. A subject is more likely to define himself based on his membership in a group than other personal reasons. This belonging can then have positive consequences for one's self-esteem, depending on the fate of the group.

Interdependence between members

A second important element for group members is mutual interdependence. Each member experiences a common destiny, he knows that his performance is by chance or deliberately, linked to that of others.

When these go into a positive reciprocal relationship then cooperation, cohesion, and greater group performance are likely; on the other hand, when interdependence negatively manifests itself, then there is competition, a reduction of mutual sympathy, and a poorer execution of tasks.

Summarizing the types of groups

In order of occurrence;

Individual: individuals united based on direct contacts, common goals, and objectives and characterized by a high level of emotional closeness and spiritual solidarity (family, group of friends, closest neighbors). It is characterized by the following features:

Reduced staff.

1. Spatial proximity of the members
2. Duration of existence
3. Common of values, norms, and models of behavior of the group
4. Voluntary membership of the group
5. Informal control over the behavior of members.

Group: a relatively large social community, whose subjects are not connected by intimate and close bonds, the connection and social interaction in the group are impersonal, utilitarian, and functional. It is goal-oriented (workgroup, school class, sports team, etc.)

By social status

1. **Formal group:** a group created based on official documents (class, school, party, etc.) and having a legally established status. The members have clearly defined positions, prescribed group norms, roles strictly distributed according to the subordination in the power structure in the group. Business relationships are established between the

members of this group, as provided for by documents, which can be supplemented by personal likes and dislike.;

2. **Informal group:** a real social community of people who are connected by common sympathies, the closeness of opinions, beliefs, tastes, etc. The states and roles in such a group are not prescribed, there is no given system of vertical relations. Official documents in such a group are irrelevant. The group dissolves when common interests disappear.

By direct relationship

1. **Conditional group:** a community of people that exists nominally and is distinguished by some sign (sex, age, profession, etc.). People included in such a group do not have direct interpersonal relationships, they may not know anything about each other.
2. **Real group:** a community of people that exists in a common space and time and is united by real relationships (a class, a production team).

Depending on the level of development or formation of interpersonal relationships

1. **Underdeveloped groups:** communities founded on social factors, lack of common goals and interests, characterized by the conformity or non-conformity of its members (for example an association, a company, etc.)

2. **High development groups:** communities based on common interests, social goals, and values (eg a team).

By importance

1. **Target group:** this is a real or imaginary group, whose norms serve as a model. The reference groups can be real or imaginary, positive or negative, they can coincide or not with belonging. They carry out a normative function and a function of social comparison. In the representations of an individual, a group can be:
    I.   "Positive": groups with which the individual identifies and, a member of which he would like to become.
    II. "Negative": groups that cause rejection in the individual.
2. **Belonging groups:** here the individual does not oppose the group, and relates to all the other members, and relates to him.

Other types of groups

1. Permanent (exist for a long time; party, school, institute, etc.) and temporary (exist for a short time; train car, people in the cinema, etc.)
2. Natural (family) and groups of psychological and another similarity (classes, parties).
3. Organized and spontaneous, etc.

The company has a very complex structure; large and small groups are distinguished in it, representing a variety of stable connections of people. A large group is a people, classes, nationalities, nations, adhering to a particular religion. Large groups influence a certain ideology and consolidate it in society.

Types of small groups

Small groups are divided into several types, depending on their size, relationship structure, individual composition, the content of activities. Depending on the design of the small group, small natural and laboratory groups are distinguished. Since small laboratory groups are artificially created for scientific purposes, often by psychologists, to study a pattern of human behavior, we will consider in more detail precisely the natural groups that take shape in society on their own.

Natural groups are of two types; formal and informal. Small formal groups are created and function within the structure of official organizations: a school class, a working collective, an academic group, etc. Informal groups are groups that take shape and function outside the official framework: friends, informal youth associations, and family. The factors on which the personal status of an individual in such a group depends are:

1. **Contact:** This refers to the emotionally favorable relationships between group members, which consist of goodwill, tact, and respect.

2. **Organization:** It is a conflict-free distribution of responsibilities in a small group, the ability to collectively solve current problems.

3. **Informative:** Each individual must know all the main aspects of the activities of the other members. The same factor involves the mutual knowledge of the characters by the members.

Group selfishness

Each small group is characterized by group selfishness, which is often a necessary element of its very existence. As a rule, the group selfishness of this small group harms the interests of another small alien group.

However, it is useless to fight group selfishness, because it is functional to make all members carry out the tasks foreseen in their activities. Group selfishness must be harmonious and not go beyond violating the interests of others. Often behind the group selfishness is the totality of the personal selfishness of each member.

In sociological research, the concepts of "group", "small group", "classification of groups" occupy an important place. The fact is that a person spends most of his life in small groups that have a strong influence on the formation of his values.

CHAPTER 2: SMALL GROUP TYPES

———— ◆◇◆ ————

The multiple and different definitions of a small group that are in circulation through the specialized literature seem to agree that it exists when there are relationships and some form of interdependence between the people who form it.

This definition, in my opinion banal, represents the maximum possible unity among the scholars who have dealt with and dealt with human groups from a psychosocial point of view.

In fact, we must not forget that there are authoritative scholars who deny even the real existence of the group, which is considered nothing more than an abstraction useful for describing a set of individuals who, in a particular environmental situation, manifest certain behaviors.

According to these authors, therefore, only individuals exist, and the group is only an abstract concept to describe the relationship situations between them in a given place and at a certain time.

Naturally, to counterbalance this exasperatedly individualistic conception there is another, equally authoritatively supported, which affirms the primacy of the group, conceived as a super-entity, with respect to the individual, who is considered a sort of passive appendix to the social grouping.

Now in such a broad horizon of interpretations by the group, it is clear that the part of the definition on which everyone agrees can only be the one that says things that are all too obvious. It is possible to list some other conditions which distinguish what is called a "small group" from other types of human groups.

Conditions that allow, with the full consent of the various schools, to broaden, beyond the banal, the part of the group definition common to the various interpretations. The small group possesses a characteristic set of properties that make it a particular case in the set of human groupings.

- Is limited in the number of components. All its members must have face-to-face relationships with each other. A small group consists of 20-30 people at maximum. Normally, however, it is made up of about ten people.
- The aims and needs of the people who make it up are interdependent.
- Each member is aware of being in a relationship of interdependence with the other members of the group.
- Relationships between people must be continuous and stable, at least for a significant period.

This list of the characteristics that a small group must possess, on which most scholars seem to agree, is interesting because it does not specify, unlike other lists, that all members must necessarily share the same purpose, but only that their purposes they must be mutually dependent. Relationships are almost always a mixture of competition and cooperation.

The group as a web of communication relationships

This very general definition allows us to understand that what characterizes both the group in the generic sense and the small group is the existence of relationships between people at a significant level of intensity and stability. Relationships are made important by the interdependence of purposes between the people who develop them.

Interpersonal relationships or interactions are nothing more than communicative exchanges between people. It is a banal statement to say that every man enters into a relationship with other men, as well as with himself and with nature, through communication. However, it allows us to recognize that the group exists only when a real communication network exists among the people who form it. A communication network is characterized by an intensity that is certainly higher than that of the communication network that interacts the person with the others who form the social environment in which he lives. A network, which conveys a more intense communication, is also more significant from an existential point of view, because it allows the people who use it to satisfy particular needs and well-defined purposes, usually sufficiently important to their life.

It is possible to develop a definition of a group that, while accepting the characteristics mentioned above, places the accent on the communicative dimension seen as a constitutive character of human social experience.

The group as a communication system

The term system indicates a set of interacting units in relation to each other. The group lends itself very well to being defined as a system. In fact, it is a set of units (the people who form it) in relation (through communication) and interdependent concerning the purpose. The group is, therefore, a system in all respects and, something more than an abstraction. At the same time, however, it is something less than a hegemonic super-entity concerning the entities that form it.

The definition of a system while recognizing that the particular aggregation of the group constitutes a new entity with respect to the people who form it, underlines that the latter do not lose their identity, their autonomy, and their freedom, dissolving as mere parts in the super-entity, as they retain their characteristic of distinct unity.

The group is nothing more than a web of relationships. The individual as such, with his most intimate and characteristic personality, does not belong to the group. Only its relationships, its communicative behaviors, therefore, belong to the group. The group is made up of people, but these do not lose themselves within it, on the contrary, in it, they realize a part of their project of themselves.

This way of considering the group is similar to the one that the great mathematician B. Bolzano used to define the conjunction "and". In his book Paradoxes of the infinite, he affirmed that the best definition of the conjunction "and" is given by the expression: "A whole composed of well-defined members".

What is the group if not a whole made up of people who is well known are well-defined members?

The group must therefore not be considered 'a sovereignty, but a system which in social life performs the same function among people as the particle "and" performs in logic.

The group is not to be seen as some sort of monster resulting from the destructive assemblage of people but, simply, a place that makes possible a series of meaningful relationships between people.

The characteristics of the group as a system

The group is an open system with the natural and social environment in which it is inserted through the exchange of information, energy, and matter. This observation cannot be omitted, with the excuse that this is an evident fact under the eyes of all, even the most inexperienced observer because it has significant implications.

The first concerns the impossibility of facing the study of the group by means of principles and laws that are based on the close relationship between cause and effect. That is, on laws which, given certain internal and external conditions, configure a group life that is rigidly determined in every detail and, therefore, widely predictable.

The logic of science has made it clear that the causal (given a cause will necessarily achieve a certain effect) and deterministic (the permanent and absolute value of this relationship) type relationships are valid only within closed systems (B. Russell).

That is, of those systems that exchange neither matter nor energy nor information with their natural and social environment. It is now well known that such systems are destined to get sick and die quickly. No human group is ever totally closed, at least its members feed on and are subject to climatic conditions that always involve an energy exchange with the natural environment.

But even on the level of information exchange, it is almost impossible for a group to be completely closed. There will always be the possibility that some of its members will meet people from other groups. This is sufficient to guarantee a minimum exchange of information between the group and the external reality.

It is clear that in the abstract it can be thought of as a completely isolated group. For example, a group of people locked up inside an atomic shelter, self-sufficient for food and energy resources. The groups of daily life, even of a cloistered type, are never in a similar condition as they maintain even a minimum flow of information with the external environment.

In groups conceived as open systems, it is, therefore, necessary to apply new concepts to replace those of a causal and deterministic type, typical, among other things, of a very mechanistic conception of science. The conception that tends to read man and his organizations like a more or less complex machine, of which, once the components have been described and known, it is possible to perfectly understand how it works.

The refusal to consider man and his groups as strictly determined and, therefore, closed systems, means accepting the bet that it is possible to understand human behavior while recognizing a considerable degree of freedom and unpredictability. This is a bet whose acceptance, however, means the willingness to fully welcome the mystery which, despite everything and fortunately, continues to accompany and characterize the existential adventure of man.

Interaction: interpersonal communication in the small group

It has been said that the group exists only because there are more intense relationships between the people who form it than those they have, at the moment in which the group is reunited, with the other people who form the social environment. So we can define the group as a communication system.

Communication is therefore what creates the group, as it is the connective tissue that allows individuals to come out of their solitude and to give life to a social organism. Communication in the group has some particular characteristics that differentiate it from that which develops within the daily life of that large group which is the social system or, more simply, society. These peculiarities of communication in a small group are because it always takes place within direct, personal, and face-to-face relationships.

Communication, which can also be defined as the exchange of signs aimed at producing common meanings, is not a "hydraulic" exchange between people. As an exchange, that is, in which a subject A transfers information into a subject B, who will perhaps respond by doing the same thing towards A human communication is something more complex and cannot be reduced to any law, however sophisticated, of hydraulic engineering. When two people enter into a relationship through communication, a sort of conflict-competition occurs between them in which the purpose of each of them is to bring the other to the terrain of their meanings.

The characteristics of face-to-face communication

Each person attributes to the signs he uses, especially in current social culture, a meaning that in many ways is subjective, as it is linked to the personal history of the individual and that of the particular social microcosm in which it took place.

Alongside this part of personal meaning, there is another objective type that is shared by all the people who use that particular language. This part of the meaning is the smallest. For example, this part of the meaning, when referring to the word "bread", is what says that this sign designates that particular food is made of a mixture of flour and water, leavened and baked. The part of the meaning of the word "bread" linked to the personal experience of bread does not appear in the objective definition because it is made up of emotions, feelings, atmospheres, sensations.

However, this part better summarizes the existential experience that the person has condensed around the linguistic sign and whose communication produces the effect of increasing the closeness and intimacy of the communicators. This part of communication, as can be understood, cannot be mechanically "transferred" in the course of linguistic communication, but must be conquered through hard work.

Interaction and parallel

Interaction should be understood as a reciprocal action, as a communicative exchange that creates an interdependence between the communicants when there is an interdependence. This effect of face-to-face interpersonal communication seems obvious and natural, yet there are communication relationships between people that produce quite different results. Here there is no subjective involvement on the part of the communicants, in which the signs remain isolated in their solitude as bearers of objective meanings and produce no new common meaning beyond that manifested by the restricted literal meaning.

In these cases instead of the interaction, there is the parallel, that is the situation in which people, despite being in reciprocal contact, act and live independently. This means that nothing of their personal experience enters the communicative exchange and, therefore, nothing of their life is shared.

Communication as a circular event

The concept of interaction highlights that communication to produce a common meaning must not be one-way but circular. This means that the communication that subject A promotes towards a subject B is not enclosed within the process that conveys the message from A to B, but expands to the return communication that informs A of the effect that his communication has produced in B.

$$A \rightleftarrows B$$

The father of cybernetics N. Wiener used to say in this regard: "I never know exactly what I said before I hear the answer to what I said." Interaction is this continuous circular process between communicators.

Parallel, on the other hand, is a succession over time of many reciprocal one-way communications. This communication sequence that does not produce interaction is a bit of a symbol of the current human existential condition in post-industrial societies. In these societies, an enormous number of communicative exchanges take place, without these being able to get people out of their isolation while preventing them from discovering loneliness.

However, the circularity of the communication is not sufficient to define the interaction. Alongside circularity, it is necessary to introduce the possibility for the communicator to foresee the effect that his message will produce in the other. The interaction postulates a minimum of reciprocal knowledge between the communicants that allows them to control the effects of their communicative exchanges. The interaction produces interpersonal knowledge.

Emotional involvement

From what has been said so far, it emerges with some clarity how personal communication, face to face, of a circular type, which is defined as interaction, takes place involving the affective dimension as well as the cognitive dimension of the people who communicate.

It deals with that process of construction of common meanings that occurs mainly through the encounter-clash of different personal experiences. The lived experience has rational contents, which are however immersed in a set of feelings, sensations, emotions, atmospheres that cannot be traced back to the logical-rational level. It can even be said that the exchange of rational contents in interpersonal communication can take place more easily within a positive emotional relationship.

Rationality and emotionality coexist within every face-to-face communication process between people. While appearing in the same act and at the same instant, the two dimensions of communication tend to express themselves in different linguistic forms.

The content is usually expressed in one of the various languages composed of a set of signs and the logical rules necessary to connect them, the most advanced example is language, spoken and written. The affective-emotional dimension, typically relational, is expressed mainly, although not exclusively, with the so-called analogue language.

In this form of language whose units are bodily expressions such as the rhythm of breathing, facial grimaces, muscle tension, tone of voice, gaze, etc. This language is not learned, except in the case of actors, mimes, and dancers. It is spontaneous and belongs almost entirely to the human capacity that is conveyed by the hereditary genetic code.

This type of language is extremely expressive but does not have any logical syntactic rules, so it can only express momentary emotional situations of whoever is communicating. This language is what man shares with other animal species. Unlike them, however, it has long since lost the ability to govern it adequately. The expressive dimension, in face-to-face communication that is established in groups, finds its most direct and engaging expression in this language. This does not mean that symbolic language cannot express emotions, but only that it does so with less immediacy and involvement than analogue language. If emotions could not be expressed in evolved human languages, neither art nor literature would exist. The discourse that is developing here concerns only the direct relationship, face to face, between people. Within this personal relationship, analogue communication performs the function of meta-communication towards linguistic communication.

It is a communication about linguistic communication, which tells the recipient of the message how to decode it. For example, if one person says to another: "How clever you are!" The recipient of the message understands whether to interpret it in a literal sense, that is, that the other expresses admiration for his cunning, or in an ironic sense, that is the commiseration for his lack of cunning, from the tone and type of relationship he has at that moment with whoever is talking to him. That is, he understands the true meaning of linguistic expression through analogue communication. This is the reason that allows us to affirm that analog communication operates at the level of meta-communication of linguistic communication when it appears together with this.

Towards common meanings

The affective-emotional dimension that develops in the interaction is a fundamental component in the creation of common meanings; indeed, it can be said that it constitutes its indispensable premise. Sometimes we agree with another person first on an emotional level than on the level of rational argumentation. Among other things, it is much easier to persuade a person with whom one has a positive emotional relationship of the correctness of one's point of view than another with whom, on the contrary, one has a negative emotional relationship.

Usually, the need to have emotionally positive interactions between group members also generates within them a sharing of meanings, that is, opinions, ideas, values, and information.

Communication does not only concern the feelings, sensations, and emotions of people, but also particular physical and mental objects on which they manifest a particular and personal orientation. This means that communication, as it is aimed at creating common meanings, also produces a common orientation among the members of the group around the contents and the object of the group work. This happens both in the case that the group has to investigate a certain problem, discussing it, and in the case that it has to make a decision or try to produce a certain artifact.

From all this, it can be seen that interaction is a very complex and non-reducible dimension within an elementary scheme. However, his analysis is the one that best allows us to understand the life of the group and that of the people who make it up.

Interaction measures of group participation and cohesion

The more the members interact with each other in a widespread way, the more the group appears dynamic, vital, and united. Counting the number of interactions that develop within it in a given unit of time is not sufficient to determine the quality of life of the group. The group in which the interactions are marked by hostility, aggression, and mutual disdain, cannot manifest itself in social life as a lively, enterprising, and solid group. Interaction must be considered the unit of measurement of the participation and involvement of individuals in the life of the group. Group cohesion and unity increase with the development of participation and, therefore, of interactions.

The term cohesion indicates that set of forces that hold together the various people who make up the group. Usually, it indicates not only the positive forces and, that is, the attraction that the group exerts on its members but also the negative forces, those that make it difficult, unpleasant, or penalize the removal of a member from the group. The interaction tends to promote cohesion based on attraction. It can therefore be said with certainty that interaction is the connective tissue of the small group, the one in which relationships are personal, face to face.

Criteria for the analysis of interactions

If it is generally true that the increase in interactions causes a greater knowledge and, therefore, a greater mutual sympathy between the members of the group, it is equally true that there are many practical circumstances of group life in which this phenomenon does not occur but in which, on the contrary, the increase in interactions causes a proportional increase in mutual hostility.

The directly proportional relationship between interaction and mutual acceptance is valid only in cases where communication produces an effective increase in personal knowledge. In cases where this does not occur, the interaction is unlikely to cause a significant increase in sympathy among group members. The cases in which the increase of the interactions does not cause the growth of mutual acceptance are mainly due to three factors: the forced interaction, the prevalence of the task, the pressures of the external environment. Let's examine them briefly.

Forced interaction

Each person has his reference value system which is usually before his or her entry into a particular group. If they conflict, the member can leave the group. If for some reason the members cannot leave the group (such as in a school class or an office) there is a forced interaction that almost always generates subgroups, made up of people with a similar reference system. Normally these subgroups develop quite evident mutual hostility.

This observation leads us to say that the interaction, to be productive of an authentic openness of the person towards others, must allow each member of the group to overcome the threshold constituted by his reference systems, which in many cases are filled with prejudices, stereotypes and selfish utilitarianism. If this does not happen, interactions produce openness only between people who in some way are already similar to each other.

The task of a process of cultural animation through the group, on the other hand, leads individuals to overcome this reductive logic of communication through the provision of group working conditions that allow each member to have authentic encounters with others and, therefore with himself.

This explains why the problem of interactions between group members cannot be addressed without exposing the role that reference systems play in hindering authentic interpersonal communication. The problem of animation is not that of forcing interactions, but rather that of eliminating the obstacles that impede their productivity on an existential level.

The prevalence of the task

Homans introduced the concepts of "internal system" and "external system" to the study of group interactions. The "internal system" is constituted by the interactions between the members of the group which is not aimed at carrying out a task but only at mutual knowledge. The "external system" is made up exclusively of the interactions that are aimed at carrying out the task.

When the "external system" prevails in a group, interactions among the members of that group do not cause any significant increase in mutual sympathy and acceptance. This means that an educational group cannot be centered exclusively on the task if it wants to favor the dynamics connected to the encounter-clash of the young person with the concrete social reality constituted by the others.

In a group centered on the "external system," the task may be unwelcome to its members. The sum of the mutual indifference, due to the lack of personal knowledge, with the unpleasantness of the task usually generates the birth of a strong hostility within the group. Prevalence of the "external system", the internal tension tends to increase. The only way the tension can release itself is through the development of the typical interactions of the "internal system".

If this cannot happen, then it is normal for hostility to develop among group members. Each group needs a balanced relationship between its "external system" and its "internal system".

The pressure of the external environment

No group has absolute control over its social and natural environment: this means that in some circumstances the environment can exert such an influence as to determine the type of task the group has to perform. When the survival of the group depends on the success in carrying out the task, the influence of the external environment becomes so strong that it heavily influences the development of personal interactions, which are centered exclusively around the task.

Even if the task linked to survival always involves an increase in participation, this does not produce any opening among the members who on the contrary, become more and more strangers on a purely personal level.

In a group that was originally formed more around the feelings of friendship of its members than around the carrying out of a task, a process of demoralization is almost certainly triggered. This situation is less rare than people think. Take, for example, a youth group of a parish community which in its time was formed more on the desire of its members to be together than on a well-defined purpose. It should be admitted that at a certain moment the leaders of the parish impose a particular task on the group, the failure of which could result in the dissolution or expulsion of the group from the community. This fact can precipitate the group in the previously described situation of profound demoralization. However, demoralization is not the only event that can happen in a group of that type. It may also happen that in the group when the problem of survival becomes urgent, a command structure tends to emerge that is not based on sympathy or ability but on the contrary the ability of some member to manage the power and exercise of authority through the use of rewards and punishments. This situation occurs much more easily within groups that have a well-defined organizational and hierarchical structure. Not infrequently in the name of urgency those with more power tend to have even more.

The staff committee, the audit committee, the report committee, the complaint committee are an example of small groups. The group may or may not have a leader assigned. Each member can influence and can be influenced.

What are the different types of group communication?

Group communication can consist of various types and mediums such as social media, print media, digital media, speeches, etc.

Benefits of learning in small groups

Flexible learning. An advantage of small-group learning is that time can be more flexibly allocated where it is needed.

- Trust that inspires
- More opportunities for feedback.
- People can be patient.
- Small groups can develop teamwork skills.
- Superior performance.
- Greater member satisfaction.

- Greater civic engagement.
- More learning.
- More creativity.
- Improved cultural understanding.

Conflict

However, it must always be kept in mind that the most effective communication model varies according to the characteristics of the group and the problem to be solved. In any case, it has been constantly noticed that people who find themselves more involved in internal communication processes tend to be more satisfied and keep their level of participation in the group higher than those who remain on the sidelines. the group has to solve our forced solution, that is they have only one exact solution, the contribution of all members to the decision process improves the probability of solving the problem, especially when the search for the solution requires diversified skills. However, when the problems to be solved have a free solution, that is, they do not have an exact and immediately verifiable solution, then the decision taken in common can be even worse than that taken independently by the leader. In any case, whatever the mechanism of the decision-making process, it seems that groups are often willing to make riskier decisions than their members individually would be willing to accept. This is perhaps because the group unknowingly determines a division of responsibility, which allows each member to reduce the sense of guilt that normally follows a wrong decision. members. After collecting and analyzing and evaluating the data relating to the problem to be solved, the group must make a choice. At this time, mostly coalitions are formed and the majority imposes its opinion on one or more minorities. This can cause tension and difficulties; therefore it is necessary to recreate harmony within the group.

CHAPTER 3: THE PHASES OF THE GROUP AND ITS DYNAMICS

———— ◆◇◆ ————

The social group is the smallest molecular entity, of a complex interactive state of roles, which constitute its atomic value. The fire and energy that allow the various atomic bonds, giving shapes to other molecules, come from the conflicts that the group produces within it is made up of symbols, myths, archetypes. Action is communicative, language, verbal, and otherwise, is the means.

The group is a dynamic entity. It has its gestation period, so it follows a development phase just like any living being until it reaches maturity and then death. The group is much more than the sum of the parts (individuals) that compose it, it is instead the multiplication of the memberships that become the exponential coefficient. Each individual is in himself a permanent assembly in continuous negotiation with continuous references to belonging and which, at times, also find themselves in conflict. For example, an individual belonging to a scientific community and researching stem cells, a Catholic practitioner. It could have already found itself in a situation of conflict, ethics, and values, which requires its resolution.

The individual therefore generally belongs to different groups that condition his relationships and outline his movements. To resume assonance with the so-called "exact sciences" we could say that: the group is the molecule and the role is the atom.

The concept of role in "Sociology" defines the set of expected behavior patterns, obligations, and expectations that converge on an individual who holds a certain social position. It is often associated with the concept of "Status" as a certain social position involves both obligations (role) and benefits (status). Each status involves numerous roles (the status of a university professor involves the role of lecturer, researcher, colleague, author of academic publications, etc.). The term role derives from the "Theater", in ancient times the actors, on stage, read their lines from a rolled sheet of paper called rotulus. The term gives a good idea of the part that each plays on the scene of society, conforming to the expectations and established rules. In most situations, we can predict the behavior of others and give our actions a consequent shape. " It is a set of shared expectations about how a person who occupies a certain position in the group should behave. Or, even better: "The set of activities and relationships that are expected from a person who occupies a particular position within the company, and from others towards the person in question.

The phases of the group

According to Tuckman, the group, both from the socio-emotional aspect and on the task-centered one, can be divided into 5 phases;

- ✓ **The forming stage:** includes dependence and orientation; members are anxious and uncertain about their membership in the group and their behavior is rather circumspect.
- ✓ **The storming stage:** involves conflicts and emotional aspects; in this phase, the members become more assertive and try to modify the group according to their needs. As a consequence, hostility and resentment erupt, as the needs of various individuals are different and collide with each other.
- ✓ **The norming stage:** involves cohesion and exchange; at this stage, members try to resolve previous conflicts and often engage in negotiating clearer guidelines and rules for group behavior.
- ✓ **The performing stage:** implies role-taking and problem-solving; in this phase, each participant works cooperatively with the others to achieve common goals.
- ✓ **The adjourning stage:** everyone begins to gradually withdraw from both socio-emotional and task-based activities. In this phase, which can be seen as a progressive disengagement, the members try to cope with the approaching end of the group. The last phase (adjourning) was added later

✓ **The evolution of the group:** a food paradigm, as we have seen, the group is structured in phases that characterize and describe a common evolutionary path.

In the initial phase, the members who will form the group, not knowing each other, begin to "smell" each other in an atmosphere that we could generally describe as anxious and circumspect. This first phase is usually very formal, static, and cold. The form of conventional communication is characterized by reciprocal formal and stereotyped presentations, describing itself also in the role it occupies within the social context of belonging.

At this stage, if we wanted to make a comparison with certain culinary semiotics by identifying the structure that characterizes the reference cultural system, we could say that we are at the appetizer. The dishes are still raw or lightly cooked, structured in shape, and embellished with decorations. In general, the appetizer directs and characterizes the subsequent courses.

Proceeding in its evolutionary path, the members begin the phase of thaw. The stereotypes are typical, the roles become more random, the value contributions begin to overlap, generating conflicts. The group, through dynamics made up of resistances and homeostatic processes, begins to outline horizons that are not yet well shared. The climate is hot.

Moving on to the culinary, we could say that at this stage we are at the first courses. Hot and steaming. Pasta or soups in broth, seasoned with various sauces and made more or less spicy and flavored with spices. In general, the first courses are consequential to the appetizers. The address could be towards meat or fish, for example.

Proceeding in its evolutionary path, the group begins to have clarity of the shared goal. He gains confidence, he moves more assertively and proactively. The phase is characterized by enthusiasm and operativeness. By sharing the objectives, the group is cemented, in the sign of belonging, on a system of shared values. The rules delimit the spaces and consequently transmit sanctions and reprimands in the transgressive acts.

In this phase of the culinary structure, we are at the second course. Second courses; Cooked, boiled. Fried or grilled. The phase is already defined and has its guideline well defined. The side dishes, in combination with the main courses, characterize the appearance and substance, giving a substantial and operational surplus to the dishes.

The circle closes with the last phase, a phase in which the members do their utmost in the formal greetings. The phase is cold and static in form and inherent in the depressive anxiety of detachment. Often redundant of aesthetically striking signs and oriented to embellish the circumstances of something that closes and for this very reason has an end.

We have therefore arrived at the dessert which for special occasions becomes a cake. Curated in form and colors. You can give space to create, but the body is now full. The more important the event is the greater the formal and redundant aspects, rather than the content ones, that will characterize this latter scope. The bitterness of the coffee and a rich and powerful liqueur will make its closure more digestive.

Understanding and managing conflict in group dynamics

Conflict within a workgroup occurs when people who depend on each other due to the nature of their work, have different points of view, different or even conflicting interests or goals. A good leader is aware that conflict is a natural and potentially productive component of group relationships and interpersonal relationships. Indeed, conflict stimulates thought, causes various perspectives about a situation to be considered, and stimulates group members to better understand the key factors regarding the decision to be made. All this when the conflict is well managed consciously and constructively.

The central aspect is not that of deciding whether to stimulate or avoid conflict, but how to manage it to make it effectively productive for teamwork. Depending on how the conflict within the group is managed it can become constructive or destructive. Effective leadership facilitates communication dynamics that stimulate constructiveness. Let's explore these two sides of the conflict in working groups.

Destructive conflict is present when it interferes with the effectiveness of the work performed and with a healthy work climate. Group members have a competitive way of communicating in which each group member tries to influence others simply to be right about their ideas, solutions, and points of view. This creates a type of " win-lose " relationship in which there are those who lose and there are those who win. The individual members of the group believe that only one of them (or a part of them) can "win" and assert themselves over the others, leading them to accept their points of view.

An evident result of these dynamics is the rapid deterioration of the corporate climate and interpersonal relationships. A context is created in which most of the group members are on the defensive by limiting the expression of their ideas in order not to risk them being aggressively evaluated (or judged with sarcasm) by others. Within these situations, personal attacks are frequent that go well beyond the content of the topic in question.

This context emerges from a type of communication that puts people on the defensive and distracts them from common goals. It is a communication characterized by evaluating, judging, the superiority of one over the other, a way of thinking and seeing things only from a perspective with an attitude of certainty and rigidity. Just as this way of communicating undermines interpersonal relationships, it also interferes with the productivity, effectiveness, and efficiency of group work.

Constructive conflict occurs when members of a workgroup are aware that disagreement is a natural aspect within group dynamics, indeed it can be a key factor in achieving their common goals. This type of attitude is reflected in a way of communicating characterized by cooperation; listening to the ideas and opinions of others with attention, interest, and positivity. Communication is used to highlight the common objectives of group members and the factors that unite them, encourages a " win-win " orientation in which everyone can claim to be a winner and this leads people to freely express and motivate their points of view by focusing on the content of the themes rather than on character or personal aspects.

To encourage constructive conflict, communication should highlight the interest of group members in listening to each other's ideas and points of view, willingness to change their perspective on an issue, and respect for the integrity of other group members and the views they represent. It is in this context that people feel comfortable expressing their thoughts and actively and constructively participate in group activities.

For these reasons, constructive conflict is an important factor for the growth of the group. It allows group members to broaden their understanding of the issues involved, enabling the group to develop a wider range of ideas and solutions. Reaching this type of context is not always easy because it is first of all necessary to overcome sources of individual pride and self-centeredness and actively seek to recognize the importance of the contribution of each person by stimulating their active participation.

The Chief's Checklist

Identify and recognize the two types of conflict within workgroups. A good leader can recognize the symptoms that distinguish a constructive or destructive conflict within a workgroup. The following are the characteristics that distinguish the two types of conflict;

Destructive conflict can be recognized based on these factors:

- ✓ **Competition:** competition between group members.
- ✓ **Attention to the benefits of the individual**: they carry individual interests at the expense of common ones
- ✓ **Win-lose approach:** decisions and solutions formulated benefit only a few members
- ✓ **Closed climate:** the group does not accept comments or ideas from people outside the group.
- ✓ **Defensive communication:** permolosity; resistance to change (group members see each new idea or suggestion as a threat to the current way of doing things).
- ✓ **Personal attacks**: individuals are ridiculed (or sarcastic) for expressing their opinions or suggestions.

The constructive conflict has the following characteristics

- ✓ **Cooperation:** group members willingly work together; actively participate; there is dialogue and mutual respect; there is an air of positivity and constructiveness.
- ✓ **Attention to Group Benefits:** Group members focus their attention on the group's goals and not just those of the individual.
- ✓ **Win-win approach:** the decisions made and the solutions identified are for the benefit of all members of the group, not just the individual or the few.

- ✓ **Open climate:** group members welcome suggestions and insights from people outside the group.
- ✓ **Supportive communication:** people are genuinely interested in the ideas and opinions of other group members and therefore actively strive to listen with empathy and provide constructive feedback.
- ✓ **Attention to content:** all opinions and suggestions are evaluated with reference to their effectiveness in helping the group to achieve their goals.

Food for thought

Think about a workgroup you are a part of during this time. What are the most evident symptoms? Would you describe how the group handles conflict is destructive or constructive terms?

Think about the company you work for. Which of the two scenarios highlighted above describes how people typically handle conflict? Taken together, could you say that the company is handling conflict destructively or constructively?

Think about what could be done to raise awareness within your company or workgroup regarding the two ways of dealing with conflict described above. Group dynamics describe the effects on the team and other members, of ROLES and BEHAVIORS that are created within a team that works together. They are therefore very important for the cohesion of the group, for the trust that is established between its members, and therefore on the results that the team can obtain.

As I mentioned in the introduction, group dynamics are about the roles and behaviors found within a team. They are therefore part of the teamwork topic. Let's see them better.

The roles that are established within a team

Within the team, there are usually ROLES. Some of these are officially established by whoever has responsibility for managing the team, while others are held "unofficially" by some members. These latter roles can be more or less functional to achieving the objectives and more or less appreciated by the other members and the team manager. They can therefore be a reason for well-being or conflict, depending on how much they are liked by others and how useful they are to achieve the established objectives.

The behavior of team members

Depending on the character and personality of the people who are part of the team, roles are established and BEHAVIORS appear. As for roles, behaviors are also divided into positive and functional to achieving positive and negative results and determining a poor quality of communication and collaboration, which generate mistrust and bad results.

The consequences of negative group dynamics

In order for teams to be effective, creative, and performing, there must be good communication within them. That is an exchange of ideas and information of good quality and quantity. Basis of positive group dynamics. But for this to happen, there must be mutual trust between the team members. Otherwise, negative group dynamics arise that lead to nothing good. When there are roles that are not adequately managed and non-virtuous-not very functional behaviors, these situations are created;

- ✓ Frequent INTERRUPTIONS from work and ineffectiveness in working on common goals;
- ✓ DISTRUST among team members;
- ✓ Lack of COLLABORATION within the team.
- ✓ Little CREATIVITY.
- ✓ Poor ability to MAKE effective DECISIONS.
- ✓ Little sense of RESPONSIBILITY towards others and the team.

The causes

Let's now see what are the behaviors and roles that define negative group dynamics. And the causes that determine them;

Weak leadership

When the team leader fails to exercise adequate leadership, a team member may take control of the situation. In these cases, the following circumstances may arise;

- ✓ Lack of clear and adequate goals.
- ✓ Conflict.
- ✓ Inadequate planning and priorities.

Excessive deference/submission to authority

This happens when team members show too often that they agree with the leader. Denoting an attitude of submission. This leads to not expressing one's opinions and therefore to depriving the team of a different and potentially useful point of view.

Insufficient exchange of ideas and information

As I have already told you above, this is the main element of negative group dynamics, a consequence of the mistrust that is generated within an ineffective team. But what are the causes of this mistrust and the poor quality and quantity of information and ideas circulating in the team? The causes are the not very functional and useful behaviors of some types of individuals that compose it. Let's see them.

1. **Individual exhibitionists-education**

   Those vain or approval-seeking people who want to draw attention to themselves in search of approval and/or recognition. In this way, they limit-prevent the interventions of other individuals, potentially useful.

2. **Eligible individuals**

   That is, those who do not participate in the discussions.

3. **Aggressive individuals**

They are the ones who often intervene by aggressively-inappropriately contradicting the opinions of others

4. **Excessively critical individuals**

   Those are always skeptical of other people's ideas.

5. **Individuals always cheerful**

   That is, those who make humor at inopportune moments.

6. **Willing to adapt to the group by strength**

   That is when the desire to obtain a consensus on the part of the group exceeds that of making the right decision. Consequently, not all possible alternative solutions are expressed and evaluated.

7. **Social laziness**

   You suffer from social laziness if you are more inclined to individual work and unwillingly participate in group work. In these cases, the work is therefore not distributed equally. Some individuals are therefore overloaded with work while others do not participate and let others do it.

8. **Fear of the judgment of others**

   Apprehension about evaluation occurs when you feel that you are being judged excessively harshly by others. Consequently, you do not express your opinions.

So what can be done in the face of all this? the right thing is to study and implement the right strategies to avoid negative group dynamics

CHAPTER 4: TRANSACTIONAL ANALYSIS IN GROUPS

———— ◆◇◆ ————

Transactional Analysis (TA), before being an individual therapist, was born as a group therapist. Berne, among his various activities as a psychiatrist, works with veterans of the Second World War by conducting therapy groups with them and developing, in that context, various insights into what would be the future Transactional Analysis.

Trying to say what the Transactional Analysis Group is would require such a study that it would be out of place here to propose. However, to have a basic idea of what the Group in TA is, and according to the original intuitions of E. Berne, we can rely on one of the contributions of the current literature in TA

The group is the elective place of change for transactional analysis. Counseling and, more generally, the consultative approach is increasingly used in group contexts. The theoretical relevance of Winifred Bion and Eric Berne's thought on the life of groups is integrated here with methodological tools on the management of groups historically matured in the context of transactional analysis, in particular with reference to the thought of Petruska Clarkson. These contributions underline the interdependence between the ever-present cognitive and emotional levels of the group. The counselor who works with groups and through groups is called to recognize and manage the relational dynamics that emerge in the function of the achievement of the explicit objective of the group. This competence is expressed in the attitude of the counselor who tends to build and restore meaning to the experience that both levels of the life of the group express.

It could be said that each person is a group, starting from the relational experiences he has internalized and which constitute the many selves that inhabit him; at the same time, every person needs a group outside of himself that feeds his vital energy through the relational exchange and meaningful presence.

Defining "the group" is a difficult undertaking any psychological and social conceptual matrix has necessarily had to deal with this plural dimension, providing each time with different perceptions and facets intent on grasping the complexity of the group phenomenon.

The place is first of all like the space-relational place that allows the birth and development of individuals, the social matrix of humanity understood both as a global set of people and as an existential figure of the human race. The destiny of men is fulfilled, as well as their script in the unraveling of events and passages of which different groups are intermediaries and witnesses: we are all born and grow up passing from one group to another, continually proposing "group stories" with protagonists notes and new acquisitions, in the physiologically ambivalent attempt to change a known and familiar writing with something surprising and new.

The group, therefore, constitutes a fundamental relational space for the personal growth of individuals, allows them to be structured in terms of personality, guarantees them an area of meaningful relationships.

It is no coincidence that professional and working contexts, public and private organizations, from multinationals to small businesses, "non-profit" realities, and the cooperative and associational world have always favored intervention approaches based on cooperation and the concept of group work conceptual and methodological bases. Those who lead groups or participate in them will be facilitated in their operational task and the achievement of the purpose if they will be able to read and manage the deep relational dynamics that inevitably characterize the life of the group.

The working group called "work team" has always been present in many public and private services, we also know that the current historical working moment suggests the establishment of groups that are built around "ad hoc" events, limited to time and objectives, due to the increasingly widespread and incentivized work for projects financed on a fixed-term basis. From a more macro perspective, the workgroup can be seen as a socially broad entity: in recent times there has been a lot of talk about " network work ", multidisciplinarity, and combined interventions between different but integrable agencies and services, which can synergistically optimize the existing resources. Often, in fact, in the psychosocial sphere, economic resources are distributed in such a way as to favor approaches and projects of broad understanding and participation.

All of this ultimately means working with and across groups: workgroups, network coordination groups, training, supervision, and counseling groups.

Counselor skills work with a coordination or leadership role within complex cooperative realities, and for those who work as a consultant and deal with training or organizational consultancy or of project.

The meaning of group living according to Berne

Transactional Analysis is perfectly realized in group therapy; or, inversely, we say that transactional analysis is a natural function of the therapeutic group "(Berne, 1961). This Bernian formulation communicates the centrality of the concept of group in the formulation of Berne's theoretical framework and even more so in its technical experiential implications.

Berne uses many clinical examples of group settings to describe his theory and devotes attention to recommending to therapists a theoretical and experiential study on group dynamics as a fundamental prerequisite for work in therapy.

So why does Berne consider the group so important in terms of change?

In the book "The structure and dynamics of organizations and groups " of 1963 in which Berne directly links, I would say almost causally, the satisfaction of the primary needs of individuals with the opportunity for participation and belonging to groups.

One of the purposes of forming a group, joining it, and adapting to it, is to prevent biological, psychological, and even moral deterioration. Few people can "recharge their batteries", to cope psychologically on their own and to maintain their moral principles without outside help (Berne, 1963).

In this sentence, there is the idea that participation in the group "guarantees" the proper functioning of all the ego states of the person ("recharge the batteries" B, "do it alone" A's autonomy, and "maintain the moral principles ", area of G).

According to Berne, every member who joins a group for the first time is equipped with a biological need for stimulation, a psychological need for structuring time, a social need for intimacy, a nostalgic expectation of modeling transactions, a provisional set of expectations based on past experience. His task now is to adapt these basic needs and expectations to the reality in front of us (Berne, 1963).

It is important to underline Berne's positive (naturalist) vision when he refers to needs in terms of "equipment", thus not only legitimizing their existence but connoting them in terms of "natural baggage" rather than underlining the aspect of lack, of the void to fill. The primary needs of people find in the group relational dimension the ideal conditions for their satisfaction. Berne, already before, in the description of social contact present in "Transactional Analysis and Psychotherapy" (Berne 1961) and later in "A che game we play" (Berne 1964).

The advantages of social contact relate to somatic and psychic balance. They are related to these factors: 1) they release tension 2) they avoid harmful situations 3) they procure "caresses" 4) they maintain the equilibrium reached (Berne 1964). The groups also perform the task of structuring time, of avoiding "boredom", in a rich and diversified way because "those who are part of a social aggregate of two or more people have more possibilities to structure time" Ways of structuring time respond to psychological needs and at the same time define the level and depth of social contact, offering "new formulas of recognition and other more complex forms of social relationship" (Berne. 1964).

The aggregate of several members, the group, is, therefore, a privileged environment for a satisfactory human experience, a sufficiently stimulating source of recognition to allow a process of identification, defined by a certain external boundary and by some internal rules such as to contain the anxieties of the loss, abandonment, the complexity of reality

The existence of the explicit objective guarantees the resistance of an object around which and for which the group organizes its culture and dynamics. The transactional analytic vision identifies the group as a fundamental resource in terms of change, a "natural" place for experimenting with relational strategies alternative to the stereotypes dictated by the life script. The group is also provided with its complexity and depth, human and relational, in which people identify themselves and from whose belonging they can derive great pleasure as well as great suffering. It is essential that those who work with groups and in groups within a consultative horizon, even in very practical-operational areas, can observe and respect this complexity, grasp its signals and nuances, direct its resources by channeling them towards evolution, above all psychological and relational, of the group.

CHAPTER 5: THE TUCKMAN MODEL AND THE FORSYTH MODEL

————— ◆ ◇ ◆ —————

The "birth" of a group, in the psychological sense, occurs under the pressure of motivations and needs that unite several subjects. Its existence unfolds over an extremely variable period of time, during which the group is shaken by changing dynamics and is characterized by the results achieved and consequently by the level of satisfaction of its members. Each group takes shape through various phases that structure its life, from its establishment to the end. These are indicative, variable phases.

Tuckman 's five-stage model

Tuckman (1965) elaborates a model relating to the "becoming" of the group which is based on the natural developmental processes of the individual, from birth to adult maturity, in particular orientation and dependence, rebellion against authority, primary socialization, maturity.

The model, the result of an accurate analysis of many previous works relating to small groups, initially envisaged four stages: forming, storming, norming, and performing brought to five later with the addition of the adjourning stage characterizing the process evolutionary through which the members of a group can, where conditions allow, equip themselves with adequate tools (structures, purposes, & roles) to successfully face their task.

The first stage, called forming, constitutes the initial phase (training period), during which the members test the relational terrain to orient themselves concerning the behaviors to be followed, the nature of the objective to be pursued, etc. It is a start-up period in which, as the target, their respective roles and mutual expectations are not yet clear, the members tend to depend on the leader, subject to more or less explicit requests on what to do, and each uses their experiences. to choose the most appropriate way to manage the situation.

The second stage, called storming (storm), owes its name to the climate that characterizes the group in the period of the conflict; rebellion against the leader, mutual hostility between the members, refusal of the task, and adverse resistance to the formation of the group. The leadership style can soften the manifestation of these "symptoms", with the probable effect, however, that the same crisis occurs implicitly and in any case not functional to the quality of the task to be performed.

The norming (regulatory period) indicates a newfound positive climate towards the group, the profusion of cohesion and commitment to make it work, the elaboration of norms that regulate the relationship life between the participants and the carrying out of tasks, the free circulation of information, mutual trust in general.

The performing (period of performance) characterizes the group, now mature, at the fourth stage, focused on the task, having now positively resolved the relational problems.

The adjourning (period of suspension) concerns the final phase that precedes the dissolution and is characterized by a certain disengagement, above all emotional, as a means to prepare for the conclusion of the experience.

This model analyzes the being of the group as an evolutionary process, characterized by the relevance of relational exchanges, whose dynamics the solution of the task becomes a function. Also interesting is the analysis of conflictual as a physiological phenomenon, to be considered for the dynamics that must not be opposed to prevent its emergence.

Forsyth model

Forsyth and subsequently adapted by Smith and Mackie (1995) appears more recent and evolved than the one illustrated above, of which it constitutes a sort of development. Also in this case the phases identified are five.

- The first has a cognitive-exploratory function. If successful, this orientation period leads each member to identify with the group.
- The second phase is often characterized by conflict, still lacking the tools to solve the problems of interdependence

relating, above all, to the decisions to be taken. Conflict often dies out when a majority is formed that persuades the group to adopt its views. Sometimes, however, it is the dissenting opinion of a minority that prevails. A single person can have radical opinions that the majority initially oppose, but which ultimately prevail.

- The third phase is the normative one, which is reached "if the group survives the conflict phase". It concerns the group that has been established, in which everyone recognizes themselves and whose value is reflected in their personal identity, to whose success therefore everyone contributes in a cooperative way, having made the rules their own.

- The fourth phase, the executive one, is a direct descendant of the previous two: in groups in which the conflict phase produces ideas of excellent quality and the normative one gives rise to high standards of productivity, the executive stage is characterized by fluid management and considerable efficiency. Individuals cooperate to solve problems, make decisions and generate what is required, manage conflicts productively and exert social influence to achieve group goals.

- The final phase concerns the "death" of the group, its dissolution, once the target for which it was built has been reached, or its disintegration for reasons related to abandonment by its members (transfers, loss of interest, need to escape the conflict)

The death of the group can be particularly negative where the phases of its life have been particularly positive since the end of the relationship reverberates on the social identity and take on the meaning of an emotional wound. The dissolution of a cohesive group can be stressful for individuals because the loss of the group involves a modification of one's identity. Members lose the benefits of the skills and contributions of others, and the security conveyed by their support and companionship. The impact can be compared to that produced by the end of an intense emotional relationship and can leave feelings of pain and loneliness.

CHAPTER 6: EFFECTIVE COMMUNICATION

———— ◆ ◇ ◆ ————

The transmission of information through the use of effective communication is today of fundamental importance because it allows you to convey messages and points of view to any interlocutor, in a manner consistent with your principles and moods.

How many times has it happened to you to communicate with someone and to have the impression of not being fully understood? We are overwhelmed with messages and information from all over, but how many of these reach the recipients clearly and correctly?

Effective communication is possible using both verbal and non-verbal language and trying to eliminate any background noise that creates both external (environmental) and internal interference. It is impossible not to communicate, which might seem easy in theory, but in practice, it requires the knowledge and application of specific strategies. Communicating means putting together, exchanging information, knowledge, needs, attitudes, emotions, between two or more interlocutors.

Effective communication: what it is and how it works

The transmission of information through the use of effective communication is today of fundamental importance because it allows you to convey messages and points of view to any interlocutor, in a manner consistent with your principles and moods.

How many times has it happened to you to communicate with someone and to have the impression of not being fully understood? We are overwhelmed with messages and information from all over, but how many of these reach the recipients clearly and correctly?

Effective communication is possible using both verbal and non-verbal language and trying to eliminate any background noise that creates both external (environmental) and internal interference. It is impossible not to communicate, which might seem easy in theory, but in practice, it requires the knowledge and application of specific strategies.

What is Communication?

Communicating means putting together, exchanging information, knowledge, needs, attitudes, emotions, between two or more interlocutors. Communication is therefore not just a one-way passage but an active exchange of questions and answers to make a clear message to all the parties participating in the exchange of information.

You can have brilliant ideas, but if you can't make them understand they won't get you anywhere. Lee Iacocca. To obtain effective communication that is able to reach others clearly, it is necessary to start from active listening. It is put into practice by remaining silent while our interlocutors speak: in this way they feel taken into consideration and more involved in the communicative act.

The goal of active listening is to be able to take the perspective of the other, understanding and addressing the motivations behind the words and gestures. In this way, a climate of collaboration and discussion is created that leads the interlocutors to look in the same direction. Try to practice active listening towards the closest people:

You will find that communication becomes more fluid and immediate, without misunderstandings.

What is effective communication?

Effective communication is effective when it takes place in a clear and assertive manner with appropriate language. Assertiveness is the ability to express oneself and assert one's ideals and principles while fully respecting the ideas of others.

Simplicity is another element that makes communication effective, both interpersonally and professionally. The more complicated the concept we want to express, the greater the need to explain it with simple and immediate language (which does not mean trivial or obvious). Communication today points to the main goal of persuasion.

It is not enough to convey a message in the most appropriate way, it is also important that this can cause positive changes in the recipients to whom it is addressed. Those who work on the web know very well that persuasive communication is of primary importance to promote or sell a product/service.

Any type of effective communication needs to be complete, concise, concrete, and courteous. Correctness is understood both from a strictly formal and grammatical point of view, and the truthfulness of the message cannot be missing.

When communication is effective

"We can have all the means of communication in the world, but nothing, absolutely nothing, replaces the gaze of the human being."

-Paulo Coelho

Communication is effective when it is complete, that is, it contains the information necessary for recipients to evaluate an offer or the possibility of a purchase, and when it serves to clarify doubts or concerns about certain problems or topics.

It is effective when it is concise (which does not mean concise) but rather centered on the most salient information, therefore without unnecessary digressions. You cannot communicate effectively if you do not support the message with concrete data and facts, based on experience.

Courtesy is essential in communication. We try to get used to using clear, non-aggressive language that respects the interlocutor and gives rise to a constructive and positive conversation.

Effective communication of great quality depends on several factors, though this alone does not lead to anything, it is always supported by other important factors such as non-verbal communication, the way in which anxiety is managed, and the tone of voice for example. To face any speech, debate, or meeting it is essential to remain calm and relaxed, to use expressions that help the process of great communication.

What makes communication effective?

'The tendency to judge others is the greatest barrier to communication and understanding."

-Carl Rogers

So let's understand together what are the processes for effective communication of quality, important points that are usually not taken into consideration because they are thought to be useless or ineffective. Quite the contrary, there are steps that need to be fully understood to be able to make a difference.

In many interpersonal meetings, the first few minutes are very important as first impressions have a significant impact on the success of future communications. When we meet for the first time we have expectations about others and so do others about us, and when these are "betrayed" here is that the first impression begins to take a bad turn, so in this case, the communication will not be effective.

It is important to maintain a sober attitude and follow all the formalities of a first meeting, such as a handshake, a smile, and maintaining eye contact.

Using the right words is crucial, if the words are accompanied by facial expressions that confirm what we are saying, as well as the nods that are made with the head, verbal communication begins to get interesting. It is often thought that to negotiate better and to communicate successfully you have to talk, talk, and talk to the point of exhaustion, even here the opposite is true.

Effective communication equals active listening

"There are always three talks behind each of the talks you have given: what you practiced, what you really did, and what you wanted to do."

-Dale Carnegie

The art of listening is a gift that few have received, active listening is an important skill that great communicators must learn to make their own.

Listening actively means understanding perfectly what our interlocutor wants to tell us, staying focused on his dialogue and deeply understanding everything he tells us with words, gestures, and the whole context that represents him.

- Be in a comfortable environment without the background noise that could disturb the dialogue.
- Be willing to listen carefully to the message without thinking about anything else.
- Do not rush to make hasty judgments but stop talking and expressing yourself until the end.
- Maintain an objective attitude.
- Don't rush to ask the next questions when an argument has yet to finish.
- At the right time, ask open and closed questions because they are important for obtaining the necessary information, starting new dialogues that lead to the result, showing interest in whoever is talking to us.
- Closed questions help to limit the answers, the answers are often a yes or a no.

Example closed questions

- Have you been to the sea this morning?
- Did you go dancing last night?
- Have you seen what the weather is like?
- Do you prefer yellow or red?

These questions when you want to communicate effectively, for example during a negotiation, are not very suitable, because they do not encourage dialogue, but they are very effective when you want to get quick and direct answers.

Open questions, on the other hand, open up to a broader and more exhaustive answer, require a different commitment on the part of the interlocutor and push him to talk more and to argue better. Open questions start for example with: Why...? When...? What...? As...? Where is it...?)

Example open questions

- How many people were there at the seaside this morning?
- Where would you like to go to the beach this summer?
- When did your professional adventure start?
- How do you see the current political situation?

It is important to understand when to close a verbal communication, the interlocutor will send us little obvious signals but it is important to recognize them. Looking at the clock several times, getting up and distancing, etc.; are signs that make us understand that those in front of us want to close the communication. Communication, as we have seen, is not simply talking and throwing words at random, but maintaining a constant balance with those in front of us to end up satisfying both of us.

10 steps to make communication effective

1. **Organize all the information**

   Often you don't take the time to organize and get all the information you need to process a conversation with one or more people. It is very important to think about the possible questions and reactions of the interlocutor to be ready with the right answer and to be able to argue any discussion.

2. **Focus on the topic**

   Concentration is everything. Often our mind begins to wander even thinking about a completely different topic from the one that our interlocutor exposes us. Staying firm on the main topic without thinking about anything else and during the conversation not talking about anything else helps not to dwell and not wander by getting straight to the point.

3. **Avoid sources of distraction**

   The background noise based on the environment where the conversation takes place does not help. If you add to this the sounds of notifications and calls arriving on your mobile, you lose all the content of the dialogue. Preferring an environment free from interference and leaving the phone without a ringtone is certainly useful for making communication effective by giving the right attention to the topic in question and the interlocutor with whom you are discussing.

4. **It catches the attention**

   As already said several times there are three levels of communication and each level weights communication;

   - 50% non-verbal language.
   - 38% paraverbal language.
   - 7% verbal language.

Simple, it's not so much what you say but how you say it. So pay attention to the gestures and the tone, rhythm, etc.; everything is communication.

5. **Be yourself**

Do not try to be who you are not, in communication it is even more important than in other areas of life. Be yourself and communicate your personality. It is important to be careful at all levels of communication without becoming depersonalized. It is important that you feel comfortable and that your message also communicates your being in the world. Ok, the technicality gives the highest priority to authenticity.

6. **Use breaks**

Pauses are an effective tool when communicating, short pauses during conversation help let what is being said affect the recipient. Plus, the breaks are even more powerful. Short breaks help you take a deep breath and breathe deeply. Especially when the topic causes tension, take the time to breathe and formulate a thought to express it.

7. **Maintain eye contact**

The look is important, maintaining eye contact helps our interlocutor to understand that we are there, that we are present and attentive to his message. On the other hand, eye contact helps to perceive all the non-verbal signals that come to us from whoever is speaking to us.

8. **Listen to the interlocutor**

Listen carefully to the interlocutor paying close attention to the words he uses so that you can reuse the same words to argue the discussion. Listening also means repeating an entire sentence to evaluate if you understand and to show that you have heard the message.

9. **Use natural language**

Formulate messages in your own words without using too technical or complex words that can make the interlocutor uncomfortable. Hardly the listener asks for the meaning of a word to understand better. Often the meaning of a word is not asked for fear of making a fool of itself, so it is better to avoid and use words that can be understood and that put the listener at ease.

10. **Listen and take note of the feedback**

During a speech addressed to one or one to many, it is important to know how to listen and accept any feedback, even when this is negative. Knowing how to welcome unpleasant feedback certainly makes communication effective by maintaining an active and constructive dialogue without either party getting upset and starting to use provocative rather than constructive language.

Communication is the key process that allows the exchange of information aimed at achieving a result. It must be borne in mind that the workgroups are made up of people who, beyond their skills, bring their baggage of emotions with them. However, a few elements of effective communication are sufficient to make communication work in a workgroup, manage the conflicts that may arise in the best possible way, and keep productivity high.

Element of effective communication

1. Use language oriented to who is to receive the message

Whoever transmits the message must communicate in such a way that it can be best understood by the recipient. To do this, we must always keep in mind that the other has a vision of the world different from one's own, and starting from this assumption, it will be easier to make sure that the message is received as it is intended to be sent, through the strategic use of questions.

Here are 3 important tools:

1. "A" Active Listening. Active Listening is an intentional act that requires a high degree of attention and communicative participation, to fully grasp what the other communicates explicitly and implicitly, as well as on a verbal and non-verbal level.
2. "B" Feedback. It serves to confirm that you have understood, received the message, and guide communication. For example, summarizing as faithfully as possible what the other has communicated immediately clarifies to the interlocutors whether the communication was successful.
3. "C" Questions. Asking questions prevents parts of the message from being left unexpressed, implied, or

misunderstood. For example, asking 'what do you think?' prompts the other to confirm whether or not the message has been received. This is also a fundamental part of active listening.

2. Talk about facts, not people. It always happens, in every project, that some error, misunderstanding, misunderstanding, or that some task is not completed as expected. In these cases, it is appropriate to examine and discuss the facts without giving blame or judgments on people to avoid closures or attitudes of defense that do not allow them to act on the facts that have produced an unexpected result.

3. Pay attention to non-verbal language. It is important to learn to manage it and align it with goals because the non-verbal language has a huge weight in exchanges between people and is considered the true source of information about the relationship. Non-verbal language is therefore capable of enhancing communication, weakening it, or making it ambiguous (due to the latter of low trust and synergy).

4. Avoid distractions. Today we are surrounded by elements that are a source of continuous distraction, mainly related to our relationship with new technologies. Therefore, silencing phones, smartphones, tablets, notifications of all kinds for the entire time of the communicative exchange will facilitate understanding and will certainly give the other the feeling of having the value of the time entirely dedicated to him.

CHAPTER 7: NON-VERBAL COMMUNICATION

———— ◆◇◆ ————

As we have seen, at work, as well as in private life, it is very important to know how to communicate. Good communication is the basis of every successful activity, however, having a good dialectic is not always enough, as communication consists of two types of language: verbal communication and non-verbal communication (CNV). Very often the second type is much more effective than the first.

The more you will be able to control gestures, posture, facial expressions, and in general all the elements of which paraverbal communication is made, the more effectively you will be able to express what you think and establish better relationships with others.

In this chapter, we will show you the non-verbal communication strategies to adopt to improve yourself and interpret the body language of your interlocutors.

But first, we want to illustrate the main characteristics of non-verbal communication and how body language is compared to verbal communication.

Non-verbal communication: main characteristics and relationship with verbal communication

When you interact with others, you just send and receive signals. The gestures you make, the way you sit down, the tone of your voice, the distance you keep with your interlocutor, are all non-verbal messages that communicate much more than your words can do.

These messages don't stop even when the conversation stops, even when you are silent, you are still communicating non-verbally. It often happens that what comes out of your mouth, and what you are communicating through body language, are two different things. Faced with these conflicting signals, the listener must choose which of the two messages to take as true and in most cases will opt for the non-verbal one.

This is because body signals are a natural and unconscious form of language that can convey your feelings and intentions in a very direct and effective way.

Effective communication, first of all, requires that non-verbal signals coincide with words because this increases trust and therefore positively affects the relationship you have with the people you are communicating with. The contrasts between verbal and non-verbal communication fuel tension, mistrust, and confusion. Here are very briefly the roles that the body's signals can play within verbal communication.

Repetition: They can repeat the message that is being conveyed verbally.

Contradiction: They can contradict what the individual is trying to convey.

Replacement: they can replace the verbal message, for example, the eyes that often convey a much more vivid message than words.

To complement: body signals can add or complete a verbal message, think of a caress or a pat on the back.

Accentuation: They can accentuate or underline a verbal message.

Types of non-verbal communication

Body language is very diverse. Let's see together some types of non-verbal communication on which it is possible to intervene to make your way of communicating more effective:

Facial expressions

Our most expressive part is certainly the face: facial expressions are capable of expressing infinite emotions without the need for words. Furthermore, facial expressions are universal; the facial expressions that are used to express happiness, sadness, anger, surprise, fear, disgust are the same for all men in every part of the world.

Body movements and posture

The way you move is also capable of conveying a wealth of information that goes far beyond words. Non-verbal communication includes your posture, bearing, the position you assume in relation to your interlocutor, and body movements.

Gestures

Gesturing is an important component of non-verbal communication, as hand movements often unconsciously accompany words during a conversation. When we analyze the hands of an interlocutor, we must always remember gestures can have different meanings depending on the culture and the country of origin.

Visual contact

Sight is certainly one of the most developed senses in man, therefore the utmost attention must be paid to eye contact; the way you look at someone can communicate many things, including interest, affection, hostility, attraction. Eye contact is also important for keeping the conversation flowing and for measuring the other person's response. But beware of misunderstandings: for example, it is taken for granted that whoever lies does not look the other person in the eye. Some research shows that liars look more deeply into the eyes, just to prove their sincerity.

Physical contact

Human beings communicate a lot through touch, think about how many messages we are able to exchange through physical contact: a handshake, a tap on the shoulder, a hug, a pat on the back, a pat on the cheek, or a squeeze on the arm. The list of messages you can give just by touching another person is truly endless.

Physical space

The distance you take from your interlocutor when you speak also communicates something: if you get too close, for example, you risk invading the physical space of the other person and arousing discomfort and hostility. If you are too far away, you could convey stiffness and coldness. There is no general rule about the right distance to take from others because a lot depends on the culture, situation, and type of relationship.

Tone of voice

It is not only important what you say, but also how you say it. If the tone of your voice is monotonous, this could annoy the listener; if, on the other hand, you know how to use the right rhythm, alternating words with short pauses or expressions that convey attention and understanding, the conversation will be more fluid and smooth. The tone of voice is also helpful in emphasizing your mood and your idea of what you are talking about.

When something goes wrong this might be the reason for disharmony between verbal communication and body language. When there is no agreement between verbal communication and body language, it can happen to send conflicting messages that fuel distrust and distrust in your interlocutor. That is why if you are unable to control your body's signals, you may have a hard time establishing stable and lasting relationships.

The reasons for this possible discrepancy between verbal and non-verbal messages are many; excessive clumsiness, body rigidity, austere attitude, denying the space of others in conversations are just a few.

How to improve your non-verbal communication

To govern non-verbal communication during a conversation, you need to be one hundred percent focused on both the verbal and non-verbal aspects of your speech. You won't be able to afford to be distracted, daydream, or think about anything else.

You have to learn to manage the stress that the communication process brings. The more stressed you are, the more confusing and unfriendly the messages you send to others through your body language. If you feel overwhelmed by stress, it's best to take a break. Only after you have regained your balance will you be able to take the situation back in hand. To improve your non-verbal communication you need to maximize your emotional awareness.

How to interpret body language

Once you have developed your ability to manage anxiety, stress and recognize your emotions, it will certainly be much easier for you to read the non-verbal signals sent by others. So here are a series of questions you will need to ask yourself while talking to someone to hone your ability to interpret other people's body language:

- Is what your interlocutor is saying in line with their body language? If you think there are inconsistencies, this could indicate that the person is unsure of what they are saying or that they are lying.

- What do the non-verbal cues say as a whole? Are they consistent or inconsistent with the words the person is saying? Reading the non-verbal communication signals individually could deceive you: therefore learn not to read the single gesture but to take into consideration all the non-verbal signals you receive.

- What does your instinct say instead? Body language belongs more to the world of feelings than to that of reason: let yourself be guided by sensations.

- Finally, ask yourself, what quality are the non-verbal cues? Has eye contact been made? If so, did it feel too intense or appropriate for the type of relationship? What is the facial expression of your interlocutor? Expressionless or emotionally present and interested? Does the tone of voice convey more heat or more tension? Are the body posture and gestures relaxed and natural or rigid and forced? Is there any physical contact? Is it appropriate for the situation? Does it make you feel uncomfortable? Is the pace of speech slow or fast? Is there a continuous flow of information? Questions and answers happen too quickly without giving time to reflect or slowly? Do the sounds you hear indicate tranquility or concern?

You will see that with time and a little practice you will improve your ability to better interpret the signals of non-verbal communication by interpreting body language, which will also be of fundamental help in the world of work. Above all, your ability to relate to others will benefit from this.

CHAPTER 8: PARAVERBAL COMMUNICATION

———— ◆◇◆ ————

araverbal communication allows you to make yourself understood by your interlocutor. In fact, through paraverbal language, you communicate your emotions, your moods, and your intentions. Paraverbal communication is usually not treated or trained. Exception made for those who carry out a job in which their paraverbal communication must be efficient such as voice actors, singers, presenters, etc.

Paraverbal communication is very important if you think about it on the phone, people form an idea of how we are through the voice we have, and in a speech, who has the most expressive voice, makes it easier to be heard.

The secrets of paraverbal communication

By paraverbal communication we mean all the characteristics of the item, therefore;

- The tone (can be high or low)
- The rhythm (it is the union of the pauses that allow you to better understand a concept)
- Time (corresponds to the speed with which we speak)

- The volume (it is what allows us to be heard even from a distance)

By working on these four aspects you can greatly improve your paraverbal language. The most common mistake made when speaking is to always use the same tone of voice to say everything. Especially in the professors, we notice this error, who often speak of something exciting but they do it in the same way they express something serious. It seems that there is no difference, but when they talk about something exciting, they used the voice with its characteristics well, their message would pass in a better way.

People use the same way of communicating in all situations. This does not allow to transmit emotions and results in a "flat" communication. As a musical instrument can play many different melodies, in the same way, the human voice has many different nuances, for example, we could;

- ✓ Speak of friendship with a voice that radiates cordiality.
- ✓ Speak about scientific discoveries with an authoritative voice.
- ✓ Discuss trust with a sincere voice.

Ultimately it is a question of discovering the possible "nuances" that our voice possesses.

One way to improve paraverbal communication is to divide the various voices into different colors, to learn how to use the right voice for the right situation:

- ✓ Friendship (the voice must convey sympathy, yellow color)

✓ Trust (empathy, green color)

✓ Authority (safety, blue color)

✓ Passion (human warmth, red voice)

1. Send sympathy

To convey a feeling of friendship through paraverbal language, the ideal is to smile sincerely and constantly. Any speech I can make without smiling doesn't have the same impact as when I smile. This type of voice must communicate availability and friendship. To create a feeling of friendship through your voice, you need to use a high volume, which is audible several meters away. The tempo will be fast, the tone will alternate between high and low. The breaks will be short. This type of paraverbal communication is especially suitable;

✓ When we say goodbye to a friend.

✓ When they introduce us to someone.

✓ In cases where we meet a person we trust.

2. Transmitting Trust

When we want to convey confidence to our interlocutor, we must use the "green voice". We use this type of voice naturally when we make a mistake and sincerely apologize. It is a paraverbal communication that reassures and creates empathy. It is the voice that a harmless and calm person uses. We tend to think that this type of voice is useless instead, it is the best for creating empathy and transmitting trust.

To create it you need to use a medium-low volume. The tone should be low, to convey the idea of tranquility. Time will have to be slow because we need to convey relaxation. The most important part in this type of voice is given by the pauses which must be hesitant (like when you don't know what to say and think about it).

This paraverbal communication is perfect when;

- ✓ You want to reassure the interlocutor.
- ✓ When you are an elementary school teacher.
- ✓ You want to convey trust.

CHAPTER 9: WORKING GROUPS

———— ◆◇◆ ————

T he goal is the purpose that the group wants to pursue and is the reason that led to its formation. No working group can be effective if the goal it has to achieve is not clear and broadly shared by members.

The target

Very often the result is not achieved due to the lack of clarity of the objective from reach. Clarity of the goal is not an easy condition to achieve. It must be possible to identify the members with the common goal, minimizing the gap between individual goals and those of the group It is about the feelings and perceptions of the members who grasp the quality of the group's environment, its atmosphere.

The climate indicators are;

- o   The support
- o   The heat
- o   Recognition of roles
- o   Openness and feedback

- **The support:** it has to do with the perceptions about the confidence to receive concrete help in case of need both from the other members and from the leader.

- **The heat:** It allows the group to work in a serene way, concentrating on the task, being able to count on the presence of other members.

- **Recognition of roles:** signals the level of acceptance and perception of individual differences. Roles tend to differentiate and enhance skills and their recognition is, for each member, the confirmation of their identity within the group

- **Openness and feedback:** they are strictly connected to the communication processes. Openness is about expressing one's ideas in the group without fear of misunderstanding. Feedback is the members' perception of the feedback information and the level of listening to the opinions expressed by others.

When there is the right support and warmth, when roles are recognized through the enhancement of members' skills and communication is open, frank, transparent, and provides clear and acceptable feedback on both behavior and results, we can speak of a good climate. But to facilitate this, it is important to create rules. Norms define acceptable or unacceptable attitudes and behaviors in that group.

In each group, there are rules such as;

Explicit: established as rules or guidelines for behavior;

Implicit (undeclared): understood as the way things "happen" in the group

Norms specify the rules by which individuals should behave, and create mutual expectations among group members. They have the individual function of being reference structures through which the world is interpreted especially in new or ambiguous situations.

They have a social function because they help coordinate activities within the group and serve to achieve the purpose. It concerns the set of shared expectations about how an individual who occupies a certain position within the group should behave.

Having different roles within the group is useful because;

- Allows the division of labor among the members, facilitating the achievement of the group's purpose (eg social and health team);
- Defines order and predictability, implies the expectations about one's behavior and that of others.
- Improves self-awareness implies knowing our role is necessary to work better.

The role

Members learn through relationships with others, what behaviors are required for the role they hold. The way of holding a position is however influenced by many factors; the knowledge that the individual has of the role, the motivation to fill it, the awareness he possesses regarding his system of skills, and by the modalities of relating with other people.

Two types of behavior in groups

I. **Task-oriented behaviors:** for example stimulate the group, seek and provide information, give and ask for opinions, reformulate, clarify, coordinate, etc.

II. **Relationship-oriented behaviors:** for example, encouraging others, observing, commenting, trying to create a serene atmosphere, favoring the resolution of conflicts, etc.

From the combination of these types of behavior, four different roles were identified:

I. **Task Specialist:** He is the one who performs numerous task-oriented behaviors, but few social behaviors. He helps the group more to follow the task.

II. **Socio-emotional:** carries out numerous relationship-oriented behaviors, but implements few work-related behaviors. It serves to create the right emotional climate and mutual support.

III. **Dual:** carries out both task-oriented and relationship-oriented behaviors

IV. **Non-participant:** stands on the sidelines

The method includes actions and procedures that allow the group to work effectively by optimizing the resources of each member.

The method can define both the technical methods of carrying out the activities (e.g. which protocol to follow for carrying out a particular operation) and the methods of interaction (e.g how to intervene during discussions).

In general, however, the method can be defined and shared by focusing attention on the question, defining some selection criteria, soliciting method proposals, and then evaluating them.

Some consequences of not adopting an effective method may be: "spinning around" in discussions and the formation of subgroups that "do something" in a chaotic way, ignoring each other, overlapping and repeating operations already performed by others.

Communication is "the key process that allows the working group to function by guaranteeing the exchange of information, finalizing it to achieve results." Communication in the group includes three plans closely linked to each other:

- **Interactive:** it concerns the relational structure.
- **Information:** refers to information regarding both work and relationships.
- **Transformative:** since it can present itself as an opportunity for novelty and change.

The communication system is defined as a "communication network" and indicates how information circulates and is transmitted. The type of network affects the behavior of the members of the group, especially as regards the accuracy in carrying out the activities (effectiveness) and satisfaction in doing so. Here are some communication networks;

Ipsilon Cross Chain Circle

In some models, the passage of information is facilitated while in others it is hindered. In the circle network, for example, each member can communicate with two close interlocutors and, therefore, the start of communication is slower because more individuals are involved. Motivation, low at first, will tend to increase because each member will feel directly involved. It is the communicative structure that gives the members more satisfaction, there is greater participation in group life.

As far as productivity is concerned, networks with a centralized structure, where one member receives and distributes communication to the others (cross and ipsilon network) are the most effective but also the least satisfactory for the people who participate in them. When there are situations of urgency, the best network is chain one because communication follows the direct route.

In general, we cannot define a priori which is the best, but you have to choose according to the task and the duration of each group. The ipsilon network and the chain network are the most effective because they are faster in communication and organization.

In the medium term, the cross structure is better, while, in the long term, the most advantageous network is the circle one which, over time, recovers productivity, improving member satisfaction.

Effective communication must be:

✓ **Finalized:** what are communicative exchanges for?

- ✓ **Pragmatics:** communication is about the collection and analysis of data and facts. What was decided? What have we produced thanks to this communication?
- ✓ **Transparent:** transparency obliges everyone to monitor and change the way they communicate with others through a high level of feedback that signals any ineffective, inconsistent or dysfunctional communication exchanges.

  Has everyone passed on all the information at their disposal? Have any inappropriate communications been reported (via feedback)?
- ✓ **Situational:** this is how communication can be defined when it is consistent with the work phase of the group. It is necessary to understand the cultural differences of the members of the group and to adapt the language to each of them, so that everyone can understand and that they also feel carefully listened to.

Leadership style

Leadership style implies that the management style must be taken into account. It exists in every group and is crucial for good or bad functioning. Leadership can positively or negatively influence the attitudes of group members. Good leadership creates a warm climate that improves group productivity.

In a group, the leader is never the only holder of modes of influence, but he is the one who has the most relevant share of leadership on a given problem at a given time. There is no single way of being a leader precisely because a different leading figure may be needed at different moments in the life of a group.

According to some authors, leaders possess certain personality characteristics that distinguish them from ordinary people; they are more intelligent, self-confident, dominant, sociable, oriented towards success, but in reality the correlation.

A good leader is also one who knows how to help the group achieve its goals in this context. There are multiple leadership functions;

- ✓ **Competence function:** it concerns the efficiency of the working group.
- ✓ **Membership function:** serves to create the right climate for which members are satisfied and work better.
- ✓ **Communication function:** oversees the image and visibility of the group, the richness, and vitality of the meetings

Here are the ways leadership is managed

- ✓ Autocratic leadership
- ✓ Democratic leadership
- ✓ Laissez-faire leadership

The best leadership must be:

- ✓ Situational
- ✓ Transparent
- ✓ Pragmatics
- ✓ Task-oriented
- ✓ Relationship oriented

Therefore, leadership is crucial to the performance, climate, communication, and decisions of the workgroup. If its function is covered with defined and clear roles, by capable people, the group will be in the ideal situation to do its job: otherwise, the group will encounter numerous obstacles.

When the aim of producing something (good or service) is set, the group transforms itself into a 'working group' which gradually tends to integrate psychological ties, as well as to balance similarities and differences, in view of achieving a target. If in the group tout court the distinctive element is interaction, in the workgroup the fundamental aspect is integration or if in a first phase, to create a group it is necessary to standardize some divergences to achieve a certain cohesion, in a second phase, to create a working group, it is necessary to negotiate the differences, integrating them without canceling them.

The teamwork in the company

The importance and characteristics of teamwork in companies have changed according to the change in the success criteria of organizations from an efficiency criterion, based on the optimization of costs and on the minimization of execution times, we have then privileged the effectiveness, with an emphasis on product quality, punctuality of execution times and response times to customer needs, and then move on to the key concept of flexibility. The latter acts in organizations at various levels (strategic, structural, operational, managerial) and is aimed at increasing integration and inter-functionality, eliminating excessively hierarchical structures, systems of production of ideas not oriented to the contributions of all, internal communication shortcomings.

Integration and inter-functionality mean for the single individual who works in the company, first of all, looking more at the processes on which one operates rather than the assigned tasks and the boundaries set by the structure, collaborating with others as part of the same team, understanding the relationship and hierarchy among the different orders of objectives, to be available to listen and communicate effectively. Integration and inter-functionality mean moving from the structural hierarchy to teamwork, or rather to a transversal organization based on workgroups and processes; from tasks to objectives (with more discretionary roles and based on professional skills), with a greater drive towards the responsibility and commitment of individuals, AND an expansion of their professional skills. The construction of the working group and the management of roles

In workgroups, there is a need for a balance between individual needs, group needs, and goals dictated by the organization. The objective is the first reference for the founding of the working group. The group has to clarify it, understand it and make it their own. People work best in groups if they know and share the group's goals, feel they contribute to the results, and can verify them, feel accepted and respected by others. The transition from interaction (group) to integration (workgroup) is achieved through the definition and sharing of some aspects of the work; objectives, methodological knowledge, action plan, resources, motivation for success. If even one of these elements is missing, truly excellent results cannot be achieved. According to Blanchard, Randolph, and Grazier, the characteristics of a winning team are a sense of purpose, open communication, mutual trust and respect, distributed leadership, effective working procedures, building on differences, flexibility and adaptability, continuous learning.

The MBTI test

The different personalities of the participants and the roles they assume contribute to achieving the results. A widely used test for group formation is MBTI (Meyers Briggs Type Indicator), created by Isabel Briggs Myers and her mother, Katharine Cook Briggs, based on Jung's theory of psychological types (1923). The tool is based on the assumption that preferences are determined by an internal disposition and typological differences produce differences in interests, values, and problem-solving techniques that can facilitate or hinder relationships between people. MBTI aims to ascertain a person's basic preferences by measuring their traits through the combination of four indices chosen from four pairs of opposites concerning energy recovery (Introversion/extroversion), reasoning modality (sensoriality/intuition), the way of making decisions (thought/feeling), the way of processing information (perception/judgment). MBTI is often used to 'map' differences within a team and to identify ways of integration between team members. Regarding roles, a study conducted by British researcher Richard Meredith Belbin) showed that it is not the participants' IQ or the affinity between their personalities that determines the success of a team. His theory, called team roles, explains that it is the right mix of different attitudes and behavioral tendencies within the team that is the determining factor of effectiveness. The roles identified by Belbin are innovator (the creative thinker of the team), integrator (the one who explores opportunities and contacts), modeler/guide (the one who seeks challenges and gets things), realizer (the one who manages the plans and ideas), coordinator (who helps team members clarify intentions and summarize what everyone wants), analyst (who analyzes and evaluates situations and things), finisher (who takes care of the details and carries out projects), specialist (the one who provides knowledge on a specific topic), aggregator (focused on creating a pleasant atmosphere and sense of solidarity). Belbin's theory does not imply that a team should consist of nine members, each with a different role. According to Belbin, the optimal team size is between five and seven members. An amusing way of indicating this same principle is that of Jeff Bezos, founder, and CEO of Amazon, who invented the so-called two-pizza rule, according to which the ideal team is composed of the number of people who can be 'fed' with two pizzas. It all depends on the size of the pizzas and the appetite of the participants!

Integration games

One of the integration games involves building a landing 'ship' for an egg as a group, making sure the egg doesn't break. Throughout the construction time of the vehicle, the participants cannot speak, therefore they need to find alternative ways of communication such as gesturing or writing. Often, in the realization of the project, a leader emerges. Participants, after finding one, are asked to reflect on the leadership process and the qualities and skills that a good leader must-have.

Another integration game involves building a bridge between two chairs or tables strong enough to support the weight of a toy car or ball. Participants have only five minutes to decide how best to build the bridge. After completing the exercise, they have the opportunity to analyze the problems that arose during the process, including the decisions made and the hypotheses discarded.

Another type of popular game involves communication skills. A participant is given a small object and must describe it to the rest of the group, who must draw it without seeing it.

CHAPTER 10: COHESION

───── ◆◇◆ ─────

Whether we are talking about work, sport or daily life, the presence of a TEAM is a VARIABLE that can improve the performance of the individual or the group. To reach the set goals, a swimmer, a tennis player, or a gymnast needs the support of his team, for a football player or a volleyball player it is essential to play in synergy with his teammates, a manager to achieve his goals needs to surround himself with people who follow him, support him and believe in him. Finally, as shown by an Australian university study, even at an amateur level, those who play sports in the company have lower stress levels, higher sports performance, and greater motivation to physical activity. Why is all this happening? Because by sharing moments, emotions, successes, or defeats, the individual's need is satisfied thanks to the group and what was previously an internal motivation for action is transformed into shared motivation towards a common purpose.

Group or Team?

Not all groups are TEAMS, but all TEAMS are GROUPS. What is it that allows the group to become a TEAM? COHESION. This variable is described as "A dynamic process that is reflected in the tendency of a group to stay together and remain united for the instrumental achievement of its goals and/or for the satisfaction of the emotional needs of its members" (Carron, Brawley, and Widmeyer, 1998, p. 2013)

Cohesion or performance?

Several studies have highlighted how high levels of cohesion are correlated with good group performance and how winning teams are more cohesive than losing teams but is it the degree of cohesion of a team that generates its success, or its success that generates cohesion? What is the right answer? Let's find out together. Several studies show this and it seems a fact that the more the team wins, the more cohesion grows, the more there is the differentiation between the members of the group, the less the chances of achieving success. If we talk about result objectives (winning or losing) the PERFORMANCE -> COHESION relationship appears stronger than the COHESION-> PERFORMANCE relationship, if we talk about performance objectives such as improving the relationship between members, favoring the development of a climate positive and trustworthy within the group, encourage assertive communication and increase the average level of the individual to ensure that the level of the group rises, then the relationship between the two variables appears circular and continuous and therefore PERFORMANCE -> COHESION - > PERFORMANCE.

Cohesion: INNATE or LEARNED competence?

Cohesion takes time. Sports psychology suggests that before intervening on the team it is important to work on the individual to trace specific skills, identify goals, willingness to learn, resistance to change, strengths, and individual moods. The secret ingredient for developing cohesion is desire. Desiring something generates "GOOD" ENERGY which is such only if it is directed towards a goal. If the group wants something superficial, generic, not discussed together, or implicit, this risks producing FREE energy and causes anxiety, disorder, and rejection within the group. To ensure that the RIGHT amount of energy used for the development of COHESION develops, it is useful to work on some skills, such as ;

- Definition of a common purpose: it allows all the energies of the individual to flow towards the team
- Knowing and communicating: listening and watching teammates
- Social availability: putting oneself at the service of the group
- Satisfaction of individual needs: recognizing the contribution of the individual within the team
- Common experience: sharing places, spaces, and objectives.

All these skills, if developed and optimized, can lead your TEAM to become WINNING, but it is necessary to work every day in a constant, attentive, and conscious way, because as underlined by one of the cardinal principles of psychology

CHAPTER 11 CONFLICT MANAGEMENT

———— ◆◇◆ ————

Managing conflicts in groups is a sine qua non for the team.

Managing conflicts in groups: how conflict arises

Conflict arises from differences between people. It is the same differences that often make different teams more effective than those made up of people with similar experiences.

When people with different views, experiences, skills, and opinions are in charge of a project or challenge, the combined effort can far exceed what any group of like-minded individuals could achieve. Common myths surrounding conflicts in the workplace and then about how a conflict can be resolved and prevented.

Common myths to dispel about workplace conflicts

1. Conflict is always negative and should always be avoided at work. When problems are hidden or disguised, they are hardly solved, consequently they turn into bigger and bigger problems. The conflict must therefore be recognized and addressed.

2. In conflicts, you either lose or win When we are involved in a conflict we take a stand based on our needs, wants, and concerns.

Project Leader, to solve his team's problems. Unless an issue affects the performance or becomes truly important within the team, a manager doesn't necessarily need to intervene.

Resolution of a conflict

The human experience of conflict involves our emotions, perceptions, and actions. We experience it on all three levels and we need to tackle them all to solve it.

The first step is certainly to recognize the conflict. The tendency is in fact to ignore the first negative signs, perhaps for convenience or fear, until these become important.

There are five general techniques for resolving conflicts. Let's see them in detail.

1. **Withdraw/avoid**

   This involves refraining from conflict situations, both actual and potential, or postponing the problem so that it can be better addressed or resolved by others.

2. **Smooth out /accommodate**

   Here the points of agreement between the two "fronts" are emphasized, to maintain harmony. You have to understand the points of view of each member of the group to manage conflicts in groups. Considering the facts, assumptions, beliefs, and decision-making that lead to the positions of others, the group will gain a better understanding of the other points of view.

3. **Reaching a compromise / conciliating**

    This method involves looking for a solution that leads to a level of satisfaction for all parties involved. Always find a solution even if it represents a temporary or partial compromise to the conflict. Once the parties understand each other's positions, it will be easier to find a common solution.

4. **Forcing / directing**

    This method is certainly more extreme because it involves imposing a single point of view to the detriment of the others. It is generally applied in urgent cases and represents a forceful solution.

5. **Collaborate / solve problems**

    This must be maintained between all members of the group It is therefore appropriate to practice active listening. All those involved, in this case, must agree to cooperate to resolve the conflict.

Conflict prevention

In addition to being able to manage team conflicts when they occur, project managers and their teams must develop ways to prevent conflicts from becoming harmful using the following guidelines;

*   Adopt effective communication and clearly articulate thoughts and ideas.

- Practice active listening, paraphrasing, clarifying, and questioning.
- Practice identifying hypotheses and asking "why" regularly.
- Don't let the conflict become personal, stick to facts and problems, not personalities.
- Focus on actionable solutions and not think about what cannot be changed.
- Encourage an open dialogue.
- Don't blame anyone.
- Show respect for all members
- Conflicts in the team remain within the team. Talking outside of any conflicts can lead to an increase in their severity.
- Addressing conflict, any disconnect or dispute can be turned into an opportunity, as well as increasing connection and trust between people.
- Working towards a solution leads the whole team to become more cohesive thanks to their common solution.
- It is possible to celebrate this moment. Even something as small as a congratulatory email or a small present to acknowledge success promotes team bonding.

In conclusion, constructive conflict, if handled correctly, can then bring a team closer.

CHAPTER 12 MANAGING DIVERSITY

——————— ◆◇◆ ———————

Starting from the second half of the twentieth century, the cultural, social, and political framework, to which we continuously refer to orient ourselves in the world of experiences, has undergone a sudden and significant change of meaning. This change has affected the internal process by which we construct the mental representations that guide our actions in the world. These changes have pushed organizational realities, even very different ones, towards the search for a new and more functional balance. Especially in recent years, men and women without exclusion of class, age, or cultural origin, have found themselves in the urgent need to redesign their biographical paths, (professional and educational) in the light of new social imperatives, contingencies, sudden changes, and of multidimensional crises that have arisen. These changes have not only affected the individual in himself but, consequently, every habitat within which he finds himself managing roles, relationships, activities, work, life. New relationship models, new family forms, new roles, and new individual functions have also invested the professional realities in which many of us invest time and energy as people at work.

Demographic changes, migratory movements, new attitudes, new expectations, changes in role, the exponential development of technology (correlated to greater and more direct access to information), represent some of the new perspectives to which we must be able to adapt and on which to reflect. Culture, values, tastes, needs, and subjective potential can no longer be taken for granted especially by those called to satisfy the demand for services: professional organizations, indeed, companies. Sensitivity towards the ethical and social dimension of work itself is growing, made concrete through provisions and new processes, renewed protocols or simple managerial and managerial attitudes translated into practice with European documents and standards aimed at fostering a culture of professions as anti-discrimination as possible and open to the increase of relational quality in the workplace. At the same time, the interest of those who invest money in organizational projects aimed at enhancing the intangible and non-financial parts of the companies themselves is growing.

The management of human potential within an organization must be held in high regard by the organizations themselves also in terms of new learning. Such an approach must aim at the production of well-being and favor the development of high-quality relationships and internal training within the companies themselves. As Reg Revans reminds us, this orientation gradually becomes an imperative, so much so that in all epochs characterized by rapid changes, organizations that are unable to adapt immediately encounter great difficulties. This adaptation would only take place through processes of learning and integrating diversity. An organization that continues to express only ideas from the past does not learn. According to this perspective, companies, workgroups, organizations, and teams cannot avoid confronting the new human concept of diversity or even better with a growing and potentially very rich complexity. Nor can they escape from examining this complexity as an element which, if taken on, elaborated, and understood, reveals itself to be the bearer of great innovation, creativity, motivation, capable of building a better general functioning. Hence, an increasing number of studies in this sense take shape and consequently find publication and subsequent dissemination.

"Diversity management. A new organizational paradigm." [Gilbert, Stead, Ivancevich; 1999]

"Critical turns in the evolution of diversity management. "

[Lorbiecki, Jack; 2000]

In the works mentioned, Diversity Management takes shape becoming a possible solution, adopted by companies that decide to adapt their internal culture to the changes taking place. The initial focus is the recognition of the intangible capital represented by the most typical characteristic of the citizens of the new millennium diversity, in fact, differences or even better individual complexity. For this reason, since the 1990s an ever-increasing number of managers, mainly Americans and Northern Europeans, have decided to adopt the philosophy of Diversity Management to "recognize" their employees and legitimize them in their uniqueness, enhancing the precious contribution that the individual can contribute to the achievement of collective objectives and favoring the increase of internal human capital and well-being in the workplace. This has a lot to do with people, with the conception they have of themselves, with the development of their personal/professional identity, and the emotional/affective dimension. We cannot ignore this if we want to reflect on human experience, regardless of the environment to which we refer. The work is carried out through the various "practices" of individuals with a personal history even before a professional one. This history potentially becomes an enrichment of the entire organization as long as it is assumed and legitimized in its being "unique, possible, relevant" and bearer of a specific potential.

The encounter with the diversity of the Other often generates critical events, often a conflict. Often the clarification of diversity, within the teams and working groups, leads to relational processes often characterized by high levels of stress and belligerence. The outcomes often turn out to be deleterious by setting the conditions for the genesis of a "stalemate"; a condition of rigid immobility, which freezes the development of work, preventing organizational growth itself. In reality, the conflict itself would be the bearer of potentially very enriching creative possibilities. When crossed in full consciousness and awareness, a crisis is capable of illuminating new paths, resources, and strategies. This also through the possible use of an intervention tool capable of supporting the group during the most critical phase of the conflict: cooperative mediation in professional contexts.

CHAPTER 13: PROBLEM-SOLVING

—————— ◆◇◆ ——————

Problem-solving can be defined as an educational-didactic approach aimed at developing problem-solving strategies and skills on three different levels; psychological, behavioral, and operational.

In problem-solving, the person is faced with a situation in many aspects and for various characteristics, is new and unmanageable according to the usual ways he has learned and known. What is therefore required in these situations is to implement a real "creative effort" aimed at identifying new strategies capable of directing us in the best possible way. This process usually takes place through a patient work of "trial and error" or, in some cases, with an illuminating intuition, a sort of insight which, by reorganizing all the elements involved, suddenly shows intuitively the correct solution.

Finding ways of solving problems that are correct and appropriate to different situations is perhaps one of the most difficult elements in the learning process. To facilitate this complex task, the so-called facilitating strategies are useful such as, for example, reorganizing and restructuring the material or data differently, so as not to fixate on old patterns of action and not to persevere ineffectively in old operating modes, but instead favor the 'emergence of new ideas and solutions. In this regard, a real "prohibition" exercise can be carried out on the use of solutions already activated previously, although these have been successfully applied.

A "typical" way of solving a problem unfolds in various phases that follow a precise "step by step" sequence.

- **Problem finding:** we realize that there is a problem to be solved that requires an immediate solution.
- **Problem setting:** we define the problem and the objective to be achieved, we ask ourselves; Where is the obstacle to my usual and habitual way of acting?
- **Brainstorming:** a wide range of possible hypotheses of a solution is defined, even those never tried before, trying to activate creativity and divergent thinking to the maximum.
- **Decision making:** after a careful evaluation of the strengths and weaknesses, the feasibility, and the chances of success of each idea, the solution hypothesis that is considered most effective is chosen.
- **Decision taking:** the hypothesis of the chosen solution is applied concretely and precisely, then verifying the results carefully and objectively. If so, we will continue to apply this solution strategy, otherwise, we will start the whole problem process all over again solving.

As you can see, problem-solving involves a cognitive activity that involves both divergent and creative thought processes (as in the brainstorming phase), and convergent thought processes (when it is required to rationally evaluate the various hypotheses and to choose the most suitable and feasible solution).

Usually, the problem solving is associated with tasks that involve logical-mathematical problem-solving skills, even if this is certainly not the only area in which it finds application; in fact, it is more correct to speak of a problem interdisciplinary solving meaning by this a better use of the skills of classification of problems and situations of different nature and typology and in the most disparate, formal and informal contexts, and of the relative ability to solve them by implementing the most appropriate strategies. The problem process solving is therefore inextricably linked to metacognitive skills of executive control of the task, such as self-monitoring and self-regulation, and tends to develop them. Below is a useful outline of the problem-solving meta-cognitive.

- ✓ Problem meta-cognitive solving
- ✓ Task/problem activity solving
- ✓ Control metacognitive activities
- ✓ Understanding

Before starting work, think.

- ✓ Is what you are about to face a problem?
- ✓ What do you know about how to proceed?
- ✓ Have you encountered similar problems on other occasions?

Forecast

Before starting the work, foresee.

- ✓ Who or what can help you?
- ✓ Which / how many tools do you need?

✓ How much time do you have available?

Planning

Before starting the task, get organized.

✓ Identify the problem.
✓ Can you work alone or in teamwork better?
✓ Get the materials and tools you need and that you will use.
✓ Choose the method of presenting the results.
✓ Establish working times as precisely as possible.

Monitoring

As you go about the task, check it out.

✓ Are you on the right path?
✓ What should be eliminated and what should be saved instead?
✓ Does the required task seem easy/difficult to you, feasible or not?
✓ If you can't continue what do you do?
✓ Is what you have identified a possible solution? It seems to you the most correct and appropriate to the context /situation you are in?
✓ Are you sure you have carefully considered all possible alternatives?

Assessment

When you have solved the problem, look back.

- ✓ Were the forecasting and planning phases helpful to you in reaching the solution?
- ✓ Did you work well and adequately?
- ✓ Could it have been possible to proceed differently?
- ✓ Can the procedure adopted in this case also be useful for you in situations and tasks other than this one?
- ✓ Was there any "catch" that you perceived as insurmountable?

We are taught to "team up" from an early age at home, where we live with other people sharing spaces, objects, affections, and rules. Then it is the school environment that introduces us to the theme of collaboration and it is precisely in this context that we discover that working in a group is not always easy.

Collaboration as well as being a way of "doing" and a working method can also represent a goal; encouraging people to give their best in a group is very different from encouraging them to achieve maximum results individually.

Let's start from a premise; creating and cultivating a collaborative work environment requires time, effort, and flexibility, which are amply rewarded by the results.

Approaching problems in a shared way leads us to appreciate the solutions, to apply ourselves with constancy and dedication to the achievement of objectives, and to strengthen the degree of loyalty towards the company. Given these premises, it is worth discovering which ideas and tools can foster and encourage collaboration in the company.

Problem-solving: where to start

"The more connected you are, the more you share and the more you collaborate" is this the case? We believe not. Conversely, a surplus of information can create chaos, confusion, and difficulty setting priorities. Therefore, it is not enough to have free spaces to have one's say, it is necessary that within these spaces the ideas are structured, ordered, and organized.

Group chats and video calls, for example, are immediate communication tools they are enough only to collect opinions, not to re-elaborate them.

Addressing a problem resolution involves;

- ✓ Know and make known the problem.
- ✓ Know the skills of individual people to involve them.
- ✓ Then make known the solution strategies so that in the future we can draw on previous analyzes for the benefit of all.

This communication process cannot be fragmented and discontinuous but must be able to be carried out in an orderly environment where the usability of information does not encounter obstacles, both technical and bureaucratic. Resources should be engaged in the elaboration of ideas, not in endless searches among disordered materials.

Solving problems together: how?

The ideal environment for problem collaborative solving must allow;

- ✓ Provide documents that can be viewed, classified, and identified correctly by the persons concerned.
- ✓ Manage relevant, easily searchable, updatable FAQ sections.
- ✓ Map the knowledge, attitudes, and skills of the staff and make them known to everyone.
- ✓ Encourage the development of interactive thematic conversation groups that can also be consulted over time.
- ✓ Guide people in solving the problem by tracking activities by phases, deadlines, and checklists shared with the people involved.
- ✓ Promote the quality of people's contributions and ideas, implementing meritocratic policies.
- ✓ Intranet platforms in the era of the Digital Workplace satisfy all these needs, guaranteeing easy access to information and its availability over time.
- ✓ The constant use of the intranet, with the consequent enrichment of documentation and thematic discussions, creates an invaluable wealth of knowledge, always just a click away.

Solving Problems Together: When?

If it is true that unity is strength, the most obvious answer would be "always" Not everyone is inclined to teamwork, either out of habit, personal, or character attitude. However, some actions can encourage and favor collaborative interaction and greater knowledge of people. Let's see which ones;

Train each other: A presentation/training practice that comes straight from Japan, known as " PechaKucha ", is taking place. There are 20 slides available to present in 20 seconds each. These short but intense training pills allow making one's interests and skills known to colleagues and given the brevity of the presentation, they can take place outside the workplace, in more informal contexts, and be the pretext for "training" aperitifs. Combining business with pleasure never hurts.

Team building: you can carve out moments in which to bring people together through "playful" activities, such as escape rooms, role-playing games, where mutual knowledge, dialogue, and the ability to communicate one's strategies are encouraged. It can also be an opportunity to overcome certain prejudices and live the relationship between colleagues more peacefully.

Participation in workshops: structuring and communicating one's ideas to make group decisions is one of the best exercises that a workshop can give the possibility to carry out. Unlike the previous two activities, usually, the participants of a workshop do not know each other: breaking the ice by expressing oneself with strangers and seeking shared solutions strengthens one's self-esteem and listening without prejudice, two fundamental components of collaboration.

CHAPTER 14: THE EFFECTIVENESS OF THE DECISION MAKING

———— ◆◇◆ ————

Why the decision in a group making more effective? And what are the practices that a good manager must adopt to organize a work team in such a way as to obtain maximum productivity in a relatively short time?

Compared to the single individual, on average the result of the decision-making process of a group exceeds the inefficiency of the most gifted element that belongs to it. In a company, it is advantageous to work in groups, or simply to get together to discuss some problems, so the correct management of these moments takes on an importance that should not be underestimated.

The efficiency of a group is the result of the interaction, discussion, and sharing of goals by its members. From this point of view, in the scale of individual involvement, certain emotional participation in the common goal is more noticeable in a team, rather than in the occasional group in which character aspects can easily emerge that tend to hinder the pleasure of working together.

Although the choice of whether or not to use teams for certain types of decisions depends only in part on the preferences of individual managers, and mainly on the organization and corporate policy habits, the reasons that push towards the choice to use groups within of decision-making generally are groups produce many more alternatives and different approaches to solving a problem than individual members alone can do, the group spends much more time researching than do individual members and has a greater inflow of knowledge than any of its members. The group offers important psychological support, useful for dealing with any pressures of the external environment; groups enhance commitment and reduce resistance to new ideas, arousing a greater understanding of the choices that need to be made.

Furthermore, given the better organization that groups can give to their decision-making activity, those factors that benefit the quality of the decision are more easily triggered; the subdivision of activities is possible when several people dedicate themselves to the same task, dividing a complex job into parts that are easier to assign to individual members; the filter effect that occurs when the group deliberately ignores some information at its disposal, to focus attention on the most important aspects of the decision, favoring the best choice, and compensation, which it is more convenient to rely on the combination of estimates of many people, rather than a single one, to mitigate the extremes and settle on a more likely average value; the adhesion that occurs among the members of the group, partly due to the sharing of the knowledge of its participants (although this is a positive factor only if it does not prevent the search for alternatives).

Managers must have a clear understanding of what is meant by the effectiveness of a group because this concept has a great influence on how the group will act and on its results. Although effectiveness is not limited to results only: it is also largely about the creativity, satisfaction, and open-mindedness that its members can express.

The main characteristics of an effective group can be summarized as follows;

- High productivity.
- Good member satisfaction.
- A high number of ideas were generated.
- A large number of problems are solved and good quality of solutions.
- The notable intensity of emotional participation.

The optimal group is composed of 5/7 members, because the smaller the group, the greater the cohesion that favors internal communication), in such a way as to obtain maximum productivity in a short time.

CHAPTER 15: THE ROLE OF THE LEADER

———— ◆ ◇ ◆ ————

We all know people who seem to have been born with a special gift, that of knowing how to direct, organize, command, order, innovate, motivate and guide the actions of others. Many characteristics identify a good leader, and in this chapter, we want to talk about the different types that we can identify in this group of people.

First of all, it must be emphasized that the attitudes of different types of leaders are based on easily identifiable pillars. For example, on the development of good social skills, the capacity for empathy (which must be balanced to ensure that it does not damage the ultimate goals of the group), intuition, which leads to being able to identify quickly and effectively what are the relevant factors such as unnecessary things, etc.

Surely all of you will have met people like these in your lifetime, or maybe you will even be one of them. But be careful not to generalize too much, because when it comes to true leaders, two fundamental aspects must always be kept in mind.

What do all types of leaders have in common?

As we just told you, there are two points to consider before identifying a person as a leader, regardless of their actions, on the one hand, not all the people who offer themselves as a guide or who is been followed by a group are those who have the necessary skills to take on the role of leader.

Like all things considered "desirable" on a social level, there are many more people who consider themselves to be bearers of the scepter of command than those who carry it. So how do you become a true leader? Is it just luck, is it a skill that is passed on to us genetically, or that we have to develop ourselves?

In this brief introduction we have not yet touched on a point that cannot be overlooked; a person who can be a good leader for one group, because he has certain characteristics and objectives, may not be so for another group. To understand this, just think of team sports.

Every week we hear about coaches being dismissed from their posts. People who should prepare a team, and who most of the time are kicked out because they have not been able to lead the group in front of them in the right way, not because they are not technically skilled, or trained in the sport of which they deal.

The problem is that there is no perfect recipe for all groups, the modus operandi that requires a certain team is not the same as that which can be applied to another group of people.

The 5 types of leaders that identify group psychology research

The English term leadership in psychology is linked to a name and an experiment: the one carried out by Kurt Lewin during the Second World War. In this historical period, we have witnessed the rise to power of several dictators, who were able to convince a large number of people to believe in their project, whether it was right or wrong.

And here we are presented with a question that might seem obvious, but it should not be underestimated, for a new leader to be born, there must be a power vacuum or a situation of strong doubt regarding the power already established.

If we continue to analyze history, we will see how the interest in the study of leadership, which initially focused on the military and political hierarchy, has then extended to other areas, such as education, sports, or business.

In other words, from the moment it was realized that leadership skills and different types of leaders can affect the productive aspect, this branch of sociology has taken on universal relevance.

Unfortunately, there is still no unambiguous classification of the different types of leaders today. To describe them, therefore, we will use one of the most practical and recognized by group psychology. This classification identifies five types of leaders, two more than those initially identified by Kurt Lewin.

1. Delegation leadership (laissez-faire)

When we talk about delegating leadership, we are referring to invisible or permissive leaders. These are people who manage the business of others and whose job is to distribute tasks. It is a particularly effective style for groups of highly motivated and capable people who are usually just waiting for someone to tell them what to do.

This type of leader makes sure that his or her directions are guidelines for the rest of the group, allowing communication. The danger of delegating leadership arises when direct intervention by the leader is required, and this does not intervene. We are faced with a leader who, if he sins, does it by default. This is why it is easy for a destabilizing element to cause everything to get out of hand.

2. Autocratic leadership

Unlike the previous leader, an autocratic leader is a person who always intervenes. His communication channel is one-way, as he only talks but does not listen to the group he is addressing. On the other hand, it is often a leader who wants a high level of control, and it works very well in those groups where people have a lot of doubts about how to do the assigned work but are already motivated. The danger of this leader is that he is not very motivated in the case of highly trained groups, because people will feel that they have lost their freedom when they go to him.

Finally, the autocratic leader often experiences a feeling of superiority towards the people he leads, an attitude that could make the balance very precarious and pose an additional danger. An example of an autocratic leader in history is Margaret Thatcher.

3. Democratic leadership

As you may have guessed, this type of leadership is the one most often applied in Western political systems. The democratic leader tries to maximize communicative bidirectionality. Lead, but don't forget the importance of paying attention to feedback from the group they lead. What characterizes this type of leadership is precisely the continuous recourse to consulting the opinions of others.

He is a good leader for prepared but not overly motivated groups. Feeling listened to can be the best remedy to increase people's motivation and interest, both in the choice of procedures and goals. An example of a Democratic leader in history was Nelson Mandela.

4. Transactional leadership

The transactional leader focuses on goals. He takes on the role of guardian of the group's motivation and, to keep it alive, rewards or chastises the people he leads according to their commitment or interest.

This type of leader, if he is skilled at his task, is excellent for leading long and complex proceedings, in which the group does not have and cannot easily find motivation in the work and in what it has to do.

External rewards (promotions, vacations, flexibility, raises, etc.) can then overcome this lack of motivation, but a good leader will need to be able to distribute them fairly and effectively.

The danger of this type of leadership concerns the objective of the project and the atmosphere that will be created within the group, in which very often competitiveness in the face of these rewards could damage human relationships. An example of transactional leadership is that of football coaches.

5. Transformational leadership

The transformational leader focuses primarily on the motivation of the group but does so starting from the task at hand. sHe intends that the group achieves its objectives, of course, but without losing sight of other "secondary" values. These cross-cutting objectives can be very different: the acquisition of skills by group members, creating a positive climate, taking care of the working environment, etc. This type of leader achieves excellent results when he has to lead a group that does not have a high level of knowledge or motivation, and that does not feel too much pressure to achieve the main objectives. An example of such a charismatic leader was John F. Kennedy.

As you have seen, the types of leadership identified by the sociological research of groups have very different and well-defined characteristics. However, when it comes to guiding and managing a group in practice, leaders don't always behave so rigidly, but rather draw on characteristics of different types.

CHAPTER 16: BE AN ASSERTIVE LEADER

—————— ◆◇◆ ——————

G ood leaders are those who never lose control, who face challenges while leaving personal problems aside, and who have full confidence in themselves. Good leaders also recognize themselves because they know how to listen and have excellent communication skills, they inform themselves consciously before making decisions, evaluating all the possible consequences and repercussions. This is why emotional intelligence plays a vital role in leadership.

Leadership is a skill that we should all strengthen because for sure sooner or later we will have the opportunity to put it into practice, as entrepreneurs, as parents, as teachers, as therapists, etc. Therefore it is necessary to take into consideration the implications of emotional intelligence regarding the role of leader and knowing how to develop the appropriate and necessary skills for this role.

What is emotional intelligence?

Emotional intelligence (EI) is the ability to understand and manage your own emotions and those of the people around you. People with a high degree of emotional intelligence know what they are feeling, what their emotions mean, and the effect they can have on others.

For leaders, emotional intelligence is essential to achieving success. After all, who will be more successful between a leader who yells at his team when under stress and a leader who is in control and calmly assesses the situation?

According to the American psychologist Daniel Goleman, who helped spread the concept of emotional intelligence, the latter has five main characteristics;

- o Self-awareness.
- o Self-control.
- o Motivation.
- o Empathy.
- o Social skills.

The greater the leader's ability to manage each of these characteristics, the greater his or her emotional intelligence.

Emotional intelligence in leadership

- **Self-awareness**

   If you are aware of yourself and always know how you feel, you will also know how your emotions can affect the people around you. Being self-aware when you are in a leadership position also means having a clear picture of your strengths and weaknesses, as well as knowing how to behave with humility.

   How to improve self-awareness?

Journaling helps improve self-awareness. If you spend even a few minutes a day writing your thoughts, you will increase your degree of awareness more and more. Try to slow down anger or other strong emotions to understand the cause first. No matter what the situation is, you can always choose how to react.

- **Self-control**

  Leaders who maintain self-control effectively do not verbally attack others, do not make hasty or emotional decisions, do not view others as stereotypes, or underestimate their principles. Self-control helps to maintain control.

  This element of emotional intelligence, according to Goleman, also covers flexibility and compromise with personal responsibility.

  How to improve self-control?

  Get to know your values and principles by taking some time to review your "code of ethics". If you know what is most important to you, you won't have to think twice before making a moral decision. Take responsibility when something goes wrong, without blaming others. Admit your mistakes and face the consequences, whatever they may be. Calmly face difficult situations to learn to react whenever they arise and manage your emotions most appropriately.

- **Motivation**

Self-motivated leaders work consciously to achieve their goals and have very high standards when it comes to the quality of their work.

How to improve motivation?

Re-examine the reasons why you do what you do. It's easy to forget what you like or why you are doing certain things. Consequently, take some time to remind yourself why you do certain things. Review and update your goals to give you the energy you need. Be aware of your position and why you are motivated. Be optimistic and always look for the bright side, regardless of the problems. Adopting this way of thinking may require some training, but the effort is worth it. Whenever you are faced with a challenge or even a failure, always try to see the positive side.

- **Empathy**

For leaders, empathy is key to managing a team and organizing goals successfully. Leaders with empathy can put themselves in other people's shoes. They help their group or team members develop their skills, challenge those who are doing wrong, give constructive feedback, and listen to those who need their help. If you want to earn the respect and loyalty of others, you need to be empathetic.

How to improve empathy?

- Put yourself in the other person's shoes and try to understand their point of view. Pay attention to the body language through which your interlocutor unconsciously reveals to you how he feels. Respond to the feelings of the other and deal with them by talking about them together, so that they always feel understood and are more receptive and open to dialogue.

- Social skills

Leaders who master the social skills of emotional intelligence are adept at communicating. They listen openly to the good and bad news, they are adept at giving support and support to their team members, especially when it comes to new projects or goals. Leaders who have good social skills are also capable of managing change and resolving any conflicts.

How to improve social skills?

I. Learn to resolve conflicts.

II. Improve your communication skills.

III. Learn to recognize the good things done by others.

IV. To be successful, leaders need to be clear about their emotions and the effect they have on the people around them. The best leader knows how to relate and work with others. Take some time to work on self-awareness, self-control, motivation, empathy, and social skills.

V. Working on these aspects will help you to better face your future and learn to manage situations in which you will have to play the role of leader, whether in the family, at school, or in the workplace.

CHAPTER 17: HOW TO IMPROVE TEAM RESULTS

————— ◆◇◆ —————

We often find ourselves working together with other people (at school, university, at work, in sport, etc.), but the activities we carry out, the results we obtain do not always live up to expectations. Ok, let's be honest; the results are often quite poor. There are inconclusive meetings in which you discuss for a long time without resolving anything, there are mediocre decisions supported only by a small part of the group, there are conflicts that tear the team apart and take time and energy away from the "real work", and so on.

This phenomenon of "loss of potential" does not only concern our group or our organization (company, school, university, association, etc.), but it is much more widespread.

"The whole is never equal to the sum of its parts," says Chuck Noll, legendary coach of the Pittsburgh Steeler American football team, "is less and less depending on how well its members work together." Let's see some useful elements to improve the efficiency of our group.

Brilliant people

The most efficient (and innovative) groups are made up of different people. A good heterogeneity allows the group to perceive and analyze each situation from a multiplicity of points of view, to process information with greater attention and awareness, and to generate a plurality of innovative ideas and proposals.

This heterogeneity must concern, transversally, the different skills;

Skills: the knowledge and experience gained by members in a specific field or discipline (product development, marketing, project management, etc.)

Communication skills: the ability to dialogue, communicate effectively, negotiate, work in a team;

Problem-solving skills: the ability to correctly define problems, an "open and dynamic mindset", the ability to generate creative solutions, etc.

If you can create a group from scratch, the best choice is to include people who are heterogeneous (and complementary) in terms of age, gender, training, skills, cultural background, etc.

If you find yourself working with an already formed group, try to bring out the peculiarities of each component; you can create an informal moment (perhaps during a coffee break) to share interests and passions, interesting aspects often emerge.

You can also take advantage of a new project to include, in the existing group, some new elements (perhaps with specific skills related to the project), which act as a stimulus for others.

Challenging goals (or "What are we doing here"?)

One of the elements that have the greatest impact on motivation in a group is the goal to be achieved. A good goal must be clear, fascinating, measurable, and inspiring.

"Increase turnover by 20% (or enrollments in our school, university, etc.)" is a clearer and more measurable goal than a generic "improve last year's performance", as well as "design and offer a unique service and innovative "is more challenging than "expanding the customer base ".

Achieving a fascinating and inspiring goal means, as Google suggests, encouraging the search for solutions 10 times, and not just 10%, better than those that already exist.

This pushes the group to think outside the box, to imagine "divergent" strategies, to propose significant changes in the various areas (product, method of use, supply chain, target customers, communication strategies, etc.) Thus, creative solutions are born that represents an absolute novelty, which makes the "product" (or service) completely different from the pre-existing ones.

Efficient working methods

What is it that makes a team truly efficient? According to Kanaga and Browning, it is the working methods and the results achieved that "confirm" whether a group is excellent. The key elements appear to be the results obtained (products, processes, services, ideas, etc.) fully satisfy (and often exceed) the expectations of customers or stakeholders; the people in the group feel fully satisfied with the process and the result of their commitment, members have gained experience and knowledge that makes their group and the entire organization more prepared and experienced in future challenges.

To reach these levels of excellence (which in my experience are not that rare), the group must learn to master some skills;

Communication: the ability to listen and value everyone's contribution, to stimulate the shyest people and to "contain" those who are excessively talkative, to share ideas and proposals, etc.

Management: the ability to recognize the elements of friction, to separate problems from people, to carry out generative negotiations, to find excellent agreements, etc.

Methods: clearly define challenges and problems, evaluate the elements at stake, overcome conflicts and build consensus, etc.

Creativity: using a creative approach in addressing and solving problems, imagining alternative scenarios, and in the creation of innovative "products", etc.

CHAPTER 18: HOW TO IMPROVE ACTIVE LISTENING

————— ◆◇◆ —————

To manage relationships at work in an optimal way, it is first of all necessary to know how to listen. Not just any kind of listening, but a conscious and attentive listening to the needs of the other; "active listening". Let's see specifically what is meant by active listening, and what are its main characteristics.

Active listening is the ability to pay attention to the communication of the other without making judgments. It is an intentional act that engages our attention to grasp what the other is referring to us both explicitly and implicitly, both verbally and non-verbally.

For it to become active "listening must be open and available not only towards the other and what he says, but also towards oneself to listen to one's reactions, to be aware of the limits of one's points of view" (Spalletta, 2011).

How to develop active listening

Be silent and pay attention

In the initial phase of listening, it is necessary to remain silent and focus exclusively on what the interlocutor is saying without interfering with one's thoughts about it.

Do not judge

It is essential to avoid expressing any judgment both on what is said (the content of the message) and towards the interlocutor himself.

Communicate our understanding

During the interaction, it is important to make it clear that you are understood through verbal and non-verbal welcoming messages. For example, you can say; "I'm listening to you", "Go ahead", and simultaneously send signals of agreement from the boss.

Avoid distractions

While listening, it is good to avoid getting distracted to consult the smartphone and the PC, or to carry out other actions that disturb the interaction with the interlocutor.

Pay attention to non-verbal communication

It is important to observe what our interlocutor expresses even beyond words through, for example, the tone of voice, posture, and facial expressions.

Rewrite the content to verify that you understand

The listener can verify what has been communicated to him through the use of paraphrase reformulation. It consists of a synthetic reformulation of the contents of the message. For example, the speaker may say: "Today I feel broken, I don't know why." The listener can respond through paraphrasing rephrasing: "Are you telling me that today you feel broken without knowing why?" The effectiveness of listening depends on the accuracy with which the listener will be able to carry out these three processes;

- Receipt of the message
- Processing
- The reply to the message

According to Thomas Gordon: "we must not confuse listening with a mere technique. The purpose of active listening is to communicate our understanding ".

One of the major problems encountered at a relational level in organizations of various types is the lack of those who hold a managerial role in paying attention and listening to their collaborators, and also the lack of "active" listening among the collaborators themselves.

This lack of active listening can have negative consequences both on a personal and organizational level, causing the onset of lowering of the levels of self-esteem or self-efficacy; episodes of stress and/or burnout; misunderstandings or conflicts at work; errors or delays in achieving the established objectives. Finally, it can compromise the image of the organization towards the external customer.

The well-known entrepreneur Marina Salamon argues that: "the inability to listen and/or communicate with collaborators are unforgivable" (Salamon, 2017).

Listening, therefore, becomes a key skill for managing communication and relationships and for developing well-being within organizations.

A common tendency when listening is to react with judgments such as; "what you say is right" or "wrong" or the type: "you are good, reliable, sincere" or "bad". If the rating is negative, we tend to dismiss the message as inaccurate or false and focus on formulating an answer rather than understanding what we are told. Often, in this case, much of what we are told remains completely unheard.

Finally, active listening is a skill that can be developed starting from the desire to understand the interlocutor and to establish an alliance. It requires a great deal of commitment and qualities of individual authenticity and acceptance of those in front of us.

CHAPTER 19: TEAM BUILDING

———— ◆◇◆ ————

U nity is strength. Especially with the people, you spend most of your time with. Who I am? Colleagues, of course! Sometimes eight hours five days a week are not enough to create effective productive mechanisms and get everyone to participate in teamwork. This is why team-building experiences can strengthen the bond and collaboration between colleagues, finally giving a human face to even the most severe of bosses. Are you ready to find out what team building is and why it works? Open your mind to a new concept of being a company, you will be surprised.

The origins: what team building is

It is from the experiments and tests carried out by the scholar Elton Mayo, in the 1920s, on the employees of the Western Electric Company of Chicago, that the first reflections based on team-building were born.

It all started almost by chance. We wanted to study the influence of work environments on people's productivity. It emerged that it is not only the context that affects the workers, but above all the company's interest in them, the consideration of their boss present to understand the progress of the experiment, but in any case, closer to people's work, involved - and again the creation of a real spirit of aggregation among the members of the same team.

Like all forerunners, Mayo was not immediately understood. It took another 20 years for the German pedagogue Kurt Hahn to materialize the same principles by opening the first experiential school in the UK.

Whether we are talking about training or corporate life, the concept of working on the well-being of the group to achieve results is what gave rise to the term we all know today team building. Its literal meaning is "team-building" and this is its essence. It is not enough to unite people in a group, it is necessary to give them inputs to create healthy and beneficial dynamics for everyone, even from the human and social side.

Team building activities serve precisely to create a shared base and to give life to a real team, destroying those walls that we all create in our minds and make real in everyday working life. And how does he do it? By breaking the routines, transporting the same people to new contexts, to rediscover each other without the constraints of the office or the preconceptions of business dynamics.

How team building works

Team building is an activity that is carried out in collaboration with professionals who deal specifically with this. Educators, event organizers, psychologists, sociologists; are all these skills at the service of businesses and corporate well-being.

To guide the participants in this experience is the team builder, a specialized guide who takes care of managing the entire activity. But beware, this is not a simple guide, but an attentive professional, who also has the task of monitoring the behavior of the people involved and directing them towards the greatest benefit for them.

The activities usually take place in open places, outside the company reality. But it is also possible to carry out mini-sessions carried out in correspondence with company conventions, to "melt the ice" among the participants, or to stimulate the growth of already existing workgroups.

The case of longer experiences is different, which can last from 2-4 hours to a whole weekend. In the latter cases, it is easier to move from the usual environments and you can indulge yourself with playful but also formative team building.

The main feature of these experiences is uniqueness, every good team-building activity is tailor-made for the people who participate, calibrated to their needs. Only in this way can tangible results be obtained and avert the danger of "losing a day", as some might think.

Does team building work?

If on the one hand, the theory can conquer everyone, it is the practice that is often frightening. Taking your employees away from work is a cost, to which is added the organizational investment. Deciding to embark on a team-building path does not mean following a trend or giving a day off, but investing in the company's staff.

With this in mind, doubts should vanish. To help you further, however, we've come up with some tips to make sure your team-building activity is effective.

Make sure all participants recognize its importance

We agree with you, it is useless to invest in those who do not believe in it. You have to do is share with your employees detailed information about the activity they are going to carry out and the purpose of the team building. Also, collect the questions and hesitations of collaborators, this will help you to review some aspects of the activities and make them even more suitable for the specific reality.

Address problems in the company before delegating them to team building.

At the base of many team-building activations, there are unresolved discontent and rigidity. If you have encountered difficulties among the participants, first speak openly with them, ask for a first comparison. Only after this sharing will you be able to propose a team-building session, in which people will no longer feel forced into an obligatory relationship with colleagues but will understand the opportunity that is offered to them.

Choose activities related to work in the company

The further you are from the corporate reality, the more effective the team-building activity is. For it to become an uplifting experience and not just a fun adventure, however, you need to make sure that the usefulness of what is being done is clear to the participants. In these activities, we play by parallelisms, but the practical intent must be clear, for the investment to turn into a real advantage.

Leave room for the participants to discuss

Too often these initiatives focus only on the activity itself. So make sure that part of the program includes discussion among the participants, to transfer what you are feeling to a practical context in the workplace.

Don't think that a single team-building activity solves everything.

When learning a new thing it is essential to repeat it so that it remains etched in the mind. The same goes for team building; you can't think that with just one appointment of this type everything changes quickly and automatically. It is necessary to repeat, to impress it in the mind and above all in the habits. Even a six-monthly meeting will be enough to refresh your memory and build a strong and united team step by step.

CHAPTER 20: HOW TO DEVELOP CREATIVITY

$$\blacklozenge \diamond \blacklozenge$$

I t is said that in 1666 in Newton, sitting under an apple tree on his estate in Woolsthorpe, an apple suddenly fell on his head, it was that event that allowed him to define the law of universal gravitation. For Archimedes, on the other hand, it was a hot bath that brought illumination to the behavior of fluids as a gift.

These episodes, halfway between anecdotal and popular myth, are based on the belief that the most important ideas for human civilization were generated by a brilliant individual in a process of analysis carried out in total autonomy.

But is this image of the creative isolating himself to find inspiration true?

The first analytical studies on the creative process date back to the 1950s initially, scientists focused their research on the productive capacity of the person. In recent times, research has evolved moving instead to another starting premise, what if at the base of the best creative results there was not a single manager but a synchronic union of several minds? Recent studies have led to underline successful workgroups, an idea that emerges from a single individual is never the endpoint of the project but is rather the fundamental starting spark to give life to someone else's intuition. Together, the team is thus able to create a result that, enriched with elements from different minds at each step, is strategically better than the single idea offered by each of the participants.

In group creativity, none of the team members are aware of what the definitive result will be from the earliest stages; the output emerges piece by piece, like a puzzle that is gradually completed.

The result is therefore not attributable to the individual because the creative process has led to the involvement of more people and ideas. Furthermore, the most performing workgroups are characterized by two fundamental qualities, the ability to listen to others is a basic element to be able to derive the construction elements of one's proposal and the ability to ask uncomfortable questions.

In these collaborative organizations, the role of executive leadership is also less predominant. In a collaborative system, the managers will have to take care of carefully selecting the members of the creative team making sure that they are representative of different mindsets; it is in fact in the diversity of the group that creativity is born, not inhomogeneous thinking.

Several studies show how brainstorming is highly productive only in organizations that, by enhancing the culture of innovation, reserve spaces dedicated to these dynamics: for example, Google asks its employees to allocate 10 to 20% of their working time to spontaneous projects and unplanned. It is certainly not possible to have an occasional meeting and hope for a stroke of genius; group creativity must be constantly cultivated.

Brainstorming can be used to develop creativity

Brainstorming is a creative technique that consists of a group debate to find ideas and/or proposals. This decision-making method developed in the context of advertising agencies is widely used for problem-solving and is mainly based on the association of ideas and comparison.

Brainstorming is a common practice when looking for new ideas and/or new solutions to problems and consists of a group meeting during which the participants discuss, proceeding by the association of concepts.

The definition of this creative technique is due to the American advertiser Alex Faickney Osborn. The term brainstorming has come into common use to indicate one of several ways to find creative ideas, but also possible alternatives to solve a given problem.

The technique initially applied only to the advertising world, is now widespread in very different fields. The fields of application include the advertising one (to develop, for example, the concept of advertising campaigns or a slogan), the artistic one (to create a work of art), the school one (for the development of a group), that of crisis management (to solve a crisis or a problem), that of the judiciary (to prepare a trial), etc.

In marketing, brainstorming is used for various reasons, including, just to name a few naming activities, creation of a logo and creation of a brand image, search for a payoff, management of projects and processes.

How do you do brainstorming or how does it work?

Before starting a brainstorming session, an objective is always defined, which is usually defined together with other indications relating to the project to be developed, in the brief, and not infrequently conceptual maps are prepared to offer starting points for reflection.

Those who have to deal directly with the work always participate in the activity, but it may be useful to involve other colleagues or people completely outside the working environment, who could provide unexpected ideas.

In any case, it is certainly more effective when done in a group, even if often, especially in small realities, this method can experiment even between a few people or even between two people and according to some by a single person. When the group is too large, however, it would be advisable to divide it into subgroups.

To brainstorm, it is always necessary to follow some basic rules, which have remained substantially unchanged over time and which can be summarized as follows;

✓ Exclude criticism (and self-criticism), because in the phase of gathering ideas it is not productive.

✓ Maintain an informal style, which could be facilitated by dedicating the first few minutes of the meeting to a very short presentation of the participants.

✓ Aim for quantity if there are numerous proposals, there is a greater chance of finding the right idea or solution.

✓ Combine the proposals already advanced into new ideas, that is, focusing on the association of ideas.

Furthermore, a brainstorming session should not be too short, to avoid stopping only on the first ideas collected; at the same time, it should not be excessively long. If it is particularly difficult to find convincing ideas or solutions, it would be preferable to prepare several meetings, lasting a maximum of one hour, so as not to weaken or dampen the necessary creative and productive energy. Also important is the place where you brainstorm, as it should encourage informality and give the group participants a chance to get up and take a few steps.

It would also be useful to prepare a blackboard in the chosen environment for brainstorming on which each participant can write down the various ideas or colored cards that can be attached to the walls.

Once the phase of collecting proposals and creative ideas is over, i.e. when the session or the different brainstorming sessions are over, it is necessary to organize everything in a structured way, correlating similar concepts with each other and creating concept maps (sometimes you can modify or supplement those previously prepared). A copy of these can be sent to all participants and then discussed in a new meeting with the aim of a critical confrontation leading to the final idea or solution.

What is emerging from productivity research is that brainstorming is a good technique that needs some tweaking to improve its effectiveness. To stimulate creativity in groups we need two promising ingredients; brainwriting or graphic creativity and electronic brainstorming, which means an electronic meeting system. Both use the basic brainstorming rules developed nearly half a century ago by advertiser Alex Osborn Faickney ;

- Don't criticize.
- Focus on quantity.
- Combine and improve ideas produced by others.
- Write down every idea that comes to mind, no matter how vague it is.

Stimulating the creativity of groups with electronic brainstorming is quite simple. It is done online using any type of online chat, such as Messenger. The only requirement is that all participants can see each other's ideas appear on their screen.

Stimulate creativity in groups with brainwriting

Brainwriting is an older technique. It involves a group of people sitting together and writing their ideas. Participants write down their ideas and place them in the center of the table for others to read. It is not allowed to speak. A new study compared the two techniques and found that electronic brainstorming produces more effective ideas.

The disadvantage of the brainwriting method is that each person must first read the ideas of others and eventually reformulate their own or other ideas. In all this, the true commitment is dissolving.

Conversely, electronic brainstorming allows each member to see what others have to say with little or no effort. This means that the group is exposed to the flow of ideas with minimal effort.

It also solves some of the problems that arise with face-to-face brainstorming. When the online method is used to stimulate the creativity of the groups, each person does not have to wait for others and stop talking to listen. Furthermore, the brainstormers do not necessarily have to be from the same country.

This probably helps explain why people in evaluations choose Electronic Brainstorming as the most satisfying experience. One last tip; research has shown that to stimulate creativity in groups with electronic brainstorming, there should be 8 or more people involved.

CHAPTER 21 CONCLUSIONS

————— ◆◇◆ —————

As we have seen, a group has the following characteristics:

- Identifiable members.
- Group conscience.
- Common tasks or interests.
- Interaction.
- Interdependence.
- Ability to act in a unified manner.

The development phases of group

- Forming.
- Storming.
- Norming.
- Performing.

Forming

- The initial feeling of uncertainty.
- Behaviors aimed at orienting oneself in the new situation, seeking points of reference, in particular in the formal leader.

- Communication is focused on rules (what to do, what not to do), behaviors (right, wrong), problems, and more generally on the general context.

Storming

- Formation of sub-groups, and the birth of the first conflicts.
- Competition between sub-groups for the "conquest of the territory".
- Questioning the role of the formal leader.
- Resistance to any form of external control.

Norming

- A phase of harmony is reached.
- "Warm" and friendly atmosphere.
- Cohesion based on the affective - relational sphere.
- Mistrust decreases and the concordance of attitudes and intentions increases.
- Behaviors of mutual support, planning, the definition of norms, objective standards.
- Meta-communication (communicating to others how you feel, what you feel) and clarification of ideas, feelings, rules, and points of view.

Performing

- The group takes on a definitive form.
- The roles are accepted and functional to the purposes.
- Behaviors are functional and problem-solving-oriented.
- Group members exhibit interdependent behaviors.

- Communication is aware and purpose-oriented.

Non-constructive behavior in the group

Dependence: the person or group going through this phase establish relationships of dependence towards those who hold the authority, even for all those attitudes and behaviors that are not strictly linked to the objectives set by the group;

Counter-dependence: this is the flip side of the addiction coin; the person or group going through the phase of counter -dependence resist authority and try in every way to question the leader;

Other non-constructive behaviors

- Aggression.
- Dominant (authoritarian) behavior.
- Manipulatory behavior (instrumental use of the relationship)
- Escape and remove from embarrassing or uncomfortable situations.
- Formation of small groups and couples of "cronies/wives".

The interdependent group is efficient and "virtuous"

The role of cohesion

The cohesion within the group is influenced by the cultural differences present between the members of the group and by other variables that constitute individual barriers (eg physical distance).

Homogeneous groups are easier to manage and are more likely to achieve a good level of cohesion. Non-homogeneous groups find it harder to unite but can become albeit with greater difficulty, very strong and united (see intercultural classes in language schools for foreigners)

The variables that can contribute to increasing group cohesion are;

- Physical/virtual proximity: working together, in the same physical or virtual place (remote workgroups) increases the level of cooperation.
- Same professional interests: those who share the same work activities face the same problems, understand the difficulties of their colleagues and help each other.
- Communication: the easier the members can communicate, the greater the cohesion.
- The number of participants: the ideal number is between 8 and 16 otherwise couples, triangulations, or lonely people may emerge.

Roles in the group

The role is what a person who occupies a certain position is expected to do; is the behavior associated with this position. In working groups, the expectations of members are related to the functions performed in the work activity.

Leadership depends on charisma and means knowing how to enthuse people to achieve goals. Being a leader of a group does not mean being a tyrant. The leader makes decisions and announces them, exposes ideas and invites questions to be asked, exposes hypotheses subject to change, exposes problems and seeks suggestions, allows the group to decide with full autonomy.

Being the leader of a group means;

- Recognize the various stages of development of the group itself
- Adapt one's leadership style with each of the members (supportive delegator - controller - manager) according to the aforementioned phases, according to the performance of the individual member, the objectives to be achieved (intermediate and final).

A group leader must know;

- The plan seeks information, defines tasks, goals, and times.
- Control keeps the group at predefined levels, makes sure actions are aimed at a goal, grasp the problems.
- Stimulate educate the group, explain motivations, maintain high levels of the group according to individual possibilities.
- Support express acceptance and encouragement to group members.
- Evaluate is the feasibility of an idea and the results obtained.
- Change your leadership style according to the person to be motivated (competence and willingness to work)

- Change one's leadership style if a person has changed his or her performance (greater or lesser competence, greater or lesser motivation)

Group development

Other roles in the group are:

- Initiator: one who suggests new ideas, redefines problems and proposes new ways and procedures to deal with difficulties.
- Information seeker: one who asks for clarification, information, and clarification.
- Opinion seeker: one who seeks not facts, but values about what the group does.
- Processor: explicit ideas and suggestions in a simplified way.
- Coordinator: highlights correlations between ideas and suggestions, coordinates the activity of the group.
- Evaluator: verifies the standards achieved.
- Energy supplier: stimulates the group.

Role issues

- Role conflict: is the result of the need to support multiple roles in the same situation (eg making the manager and spouse attentive to family needs).
- Role incompatibility: when competing expectations exist for the same role (e.g. group leader caught between expectations of superior and group members).

- Role overload: when a person has too many roles to manage (eg being a friend, boss, technician, etc.)
- Role underestimation: when an individual is assigned a role that diminishes self-concept.
- Role ambiguity: when there is no certainty about the assigned role.

Internal tensions

- Tension in the group is a latent (hidden) and collective emotional state that disturbs the work and harmony of the group.
- A tension can express itself in the form of a conflict of opinion. But systematically avoiding conflicts of ideas leads the group to sterility and banality. The group does not progress without contrasts and comparisons.
- Not all tensions are therefore negative.
- Negative tension is a state of non-evident dissatisfaction suffered by the members of the group which blocks the progress of the group and which explodes in crisis or discharge of tension.

The most frequent types of voltage are;

- Tensions due to latent or declared conflicts. They are due to insecurity or leadership conflicts.
- Tensions due to the group's opposition to its boss results in discontent and irritation.
- Release of tension is a temporary solution that allows a momentary relief to the discomfort of a group. It can be

manifested by irrepressible laughter, verbal aggression, and unexpected anger.

- Unloading tension does not always resolve the tension, which will reproduce itself more or less quickly.
- The real solution will only come when the tension becomes manifest (and not latent) and is discussed and treated with a suitable method. Out of a kind of fear of risks, the group always tries to deny the tensions and release them rather than analyze them.
- The lack of tension and cohesion influences the morale of the latter.

The characteristics that contribute to keeping the morale of the group high are;

- The good performance of interpersonal effective relationships creates satisfaction.
- Towards members, mutual help, cohesion, mutual understanding, and trust.
- The good progress of relations with the formal authority corresponds to trust in the head and the absence of conflicts due to rivalry.
- Confidence in the accessibility of the group's objectives corresponds to confidence in the ability of the group and in the future realization of the objectives.
- The tolerance of external constraints and pressures reinforces the defensive cohesion of the group. The group

unites against any external pressures and strengthens its solidarity.

- A positive environment makes the group the center of attraction and expresses the satisfaction of belonging to it.

- The ideal workgroup is the one that succeeds a good balance between individual and group goals; orientation to the relationship (quality of personal relationships) and the task (professional objectives); cooperation and individual autonomy.

- One of the members can, at any time, leave the group temporarily (maternity, vacation, accident, refresher course, etc) or permanently (dissatisfaction, change of group, change of job, retirement, etc). Therefore the leader (formal or effective) must make sure that this removal does not preclude the achievement of the objectives and the well-being of the other members. Therefore the interchangeability of the various roles must be pursued. Everyone must understand that the group MUST continue to function even in the absence of one of the members.

In all this, we have seen what an important role communication has, how communicating effectively is fundamental for the very existence and functionality of the group. All members must communicate clearly and openly with each other in order not to create jealousies and misunderstandings that could undermine the purpose of the group. For these, all members of the group should learn to communicate effectively in an assertive way, in such a way as to avoid both aggressive attitudes that exacerbate disagreements within the group, and passive behaviors, which create apathy and do not allow to reach the goal the final.

Living and working in groups and organizations is not always easy. In each team, people with different histories, attitudes, and passions take on the non-trivial task of rowing together hopefully as pleasantly and productively as possible in the same direction. To do this, they must necessarily learn to confront and interact openly and effectively, overcoming misunderstandings, frictions, and sometimes different points of view. That is, they must accept the challenge of creating constructive relationships with others. For this reason, developing emotional intelligence that is, the ability to manage emotions as a group is a key step in working relationships.

What I can recommend to those who want to improve their way of being a group is to start observing and identifying the typical behaviors of those who interact fruitfully in their teamwork.

Among all, I present to you what, in my opinion, are the 10 most important and relevant attitudes to make the group work well.

1. Ask questions and encourage the other to speak, ask for feedback from others, accept points of view different from one's own.

2. Express their opinions or points of view, uphold their rights, speak in first person and directly, affirming needs, expectations, desires, that is, clarifying to oneself and others what one wants to achieve; express doubts, criticisms, or compliments.

3. Evaluate the criticisms received before reacting; seek suggestions, recognize your mistakes.

4. Taking responsibility for the result of the group; try to "solve the problem" instead of "look for the culprit".

5. Facing problems and organizing work together with others, without isolating oneself; collaborate and share decisions to be made with others.

6. Promote the development of a peaceful climate; instill confidence, joy, and well-being in the environment in which one lives.

7. Encourage, enhance and "reward" the results of one's workgroup/protect the group and its reputation, share one's merits with others.

8. Change behavior, strategy, or contact person depending on the situation.

9. Questioning one's position and/or one's ideas; adapt their behavior and change their opinions to more information received.

10. Identify and propose different choice/behavior alternatives that interest the interlocutor or the group.

www.ingramcontent.com/pod-product-compliance
Lightning Source LLC
Chambersburg PA
CBHW071417210326
41597CB00020B/3537

9 781778 186004